ROGER G. K. PENN

Memories of Sarah Jane Howell

A Welsh Heroine

To Angela
All good wishes
Thank for visiting us for
on Cream Tea Wed 4/8/21

Roger

Published by Penn-manship Projects
Dolycwrt, Whitland, Carmarthenshire.

ISBN 978-0-9931313-0-1

Printed and bound in Wales
by Dinefwr Press, Llandybie, Carmarthenshire.

*This work is dedicated to
my wife, Celeste, a source of
loving help and support, always.*

Contents

Thanks and Acknowledgements

IN DECEMBER 2011, I was privileged to attend the centenary memorial service commemorating Sarah Jane's act of bravery which resulted in the tragic circumstances of her drowning. In the friendly environment of Brynmenyn School Central Hall, amongst children, teachers, governors and guests, it was touching for me to experience the respect that is still afforded to my great aunt after all these years. Now that I have been fortunate to complete Sarah Jane's story, I would like to thank everyone who has helped me along the way.

Sarah Jane's life began in 1890, at a time when *The Central Glamorgan Gazette* was reporting the news of a rather different Brynmenyn and Bridgend from what we know today. In truth, this publication, later known as *The Glamorgan Gazette,* which continues to enrich the lives of present-day readers, provided the necessary background details for me to tackle the work. In offering sincere thanks to everyone associated with the newspaper I would like to give a special mention to Lesley Milne, Theresa Saunders and John Dunkley-Williams at Bridgend Reference Library where the records are available on microfilm, amongst other historical papers and documents.

In the course of my research, I have also referred to the *Western Mail*, the *South Wales Daily News*, *The Herald* (of

Wales), *The Clifton Chronicle* and *The Bath Chronicle*. This has meant visiting the Central Libraries of Carmarthen, Swansea, Cardiff and Bristol, as well as the Glamorgan Archives in Cardiff, besides corresponding with librarians in Bath, Swindon and the National Library of Wales. I have also been assisted by the staff of Registry Offices in Tredegar, Bridgend, Bath and Swindon, and volunteers at the Aberkenfig Resource Centre. Thank you all very much.

In compiling this story, I have had the pleasure of being invited to view old records belonging to Clifton High School by kind permission of Dr Alison Neill, Head of the School, in the belief that both my great aunt and her sister, my grandmother, Beatrice, had once been pupils there. As it transpired, however, they were educated a short distance from this famous place of learning which, nevertheless, offered me an insight into earlier boarding school life in Bristol, for which I thank Dr Neill and her staff, particularly Emily Freire-Banos.

Whilst on my travels, I also had the pleasure of meeting two gentlemen, Tom Harry and Meurig O'Connor, who provided first-hand knowledge of the leading social events taking place during Sarah Jane's days. Meurig, who recently died at the age of one-hundred-and-three, was a popular character in Cowbridge and the details of his early life never left his memory. As for Tom, he shared ideas with me that have enriched the book, for which I am grateful.

In providing photographs to support the story, I wish to thank Wyndham Jones and Leslie Allen of Gilfach Goch, Dawn Osborne, Tim Midwinter, Dr Alison Neill, Peter

Evans, my sister Elizabeth Bevan, and my late father's cousin, Janet Moody of Whitchurch, Cardiff. Indeed, I am indebted to Janet for making available her press cuttings and memorabilia concerning Sarah Jane, as well as passing on details of earlier day-to-day life within the Howell family. Janet is the daughter of Katie, the second born of the six Howell girls and Sarah Jane's closest friend; and it is she who explained that the sisters changed their name from 'Howells' (their father being born George Howells) to 'Howell,' a small detail that needs clarification. Within the family, I also owe so much to my late grandmother, Beatrice, another of Sarah Jane's sisters, who over the years told me about her own schooling in Clifton, without me realising how useful this information might be.

I would like to thank Mrs Clare Dale, the present Head Teacher of Brynmenyn Primary School and her colleagues and governors, including predecessors, for continuing to respect Sarah Jane's act of heroism. I know that Mr Islwyn Thomas, former Headmaster, with the help of past-pupil Lynette Daniel and also Linda Jones of the Glamorgan Family History Society, worked hard to assemble a Sarah Jane file at the school, which has been helpful to me; diolch yn fawr i chi gyd. Brynmenyn School was opened on January 13th 1913 and Sarah Jane once looked forward to teaching there. Now, over one hundred years later, today's same establishment, which appears to have altered little since that earlier date, has celebrated its own centenary and, for this reason, I have incorporated into the story a few of the school's treasured memories from the past.

I would like to thank Lesley Milne and Tom Harry, mentioned earlier, and Wally Rainbow for reading my book, and Meurig Davies and Mair Mathias, both of Whitland, for helping me to translate Welsh hymns mentioned in the story. Finally, I wish to extend my appreciation to the people who gave me direction and local knowledge when I arrived on their streets to track-down the earlier movements of my great aunt. I refer to the good people of Brynmenyn, Tondu, Llangeinor, Gilfach Goch and the surrounding villages. Thank you all.

As always, turning a piece of writing into a marketable publication cannot happen without the professional assistance of others. This volume is no exception and I am grateful for the support I received. I refer to Andy Ellis of the Writer's Bureau in Manchester; Penny Legg, an author and freelance editor; Ritchie Craven, Publications manager for the Church in Wales; members of the Welsh Books Council and, finally, both Dinefwr Printers and Gwasg Gomer Press for taking my work into the homes of readers. Diolch yn fawr am gymryd diddordeb yn y stori ac am rhoi help i fi yn llawn.

Now, it only remains for me to thank everyone for opening the pages of this little book. I sincerely hope you enjoy the journey into the world once known by Sarah Jane.

Roger Penn
Dolycwrt, Whitland
August 2014

Foreword

WHEN I ARRIVED at Brynmenyn Primary School in 2005, I can remember being taken aside by Islwyn Thomas, headmaster, and being enlightened by all I heard about Sarah Jane Howell. At the time I knew nothing about her bravery and courage way back in 1911, yet I immediately began to understand the fullness of her personal legacy to our school.

Islwyn spoke of the children's passion for the story and their fascination for Bertie Gubbins following the fateful day when Sarah Jane drowned. He also explained that for years a beautiful memorial sculpture honoured Sarah Jane outside the school, until it was torn away, never to be seen again.

I believe that there can be no greater testimony to Sarah Jane's popularity and respect than the presentation of an annual award in her name to the best scholar at Brynmenyn. This is always an occasion of fun, happiness and reflection that pupils, staff, governors and parents look forward to.

I am delighted to see the completion of this story which, structured into an easy read, offers an intriguing study of Sarah Jane against background details relevant to her time. I am sure that the book will be enjoyed by everyone in the locality as well as lovers of history, tradition and heroism further afield.

H Clare Dale
Head Teacher, Brynmenyn Primary School
2014

Preface

SARAH JANE HOWELL was the eldest of six daughters to be raised at Abergarw farm, Brynmenyn, near Bridgend. Born in 1890 into a world of country life, Sarah Jane became a fashionable young lady whose shy nature embraced an easy charm. As an elementary school teacher she was much loved, and her bright future brought the world to her feet.

But on the morning of Tuesday, December 19th 1911 disaster struck. Whilst walking with her pupils towards Brynmenyn Council School, Sarah Jane drowned trying to rescue a small boy who had slipped into the Llynfi river.

This untimely death left a village and a community in sadness and a family in despair, but the young heroine has never been forgotten. To this day, the annual *Sarah Jane Howell Award* at Brynmenyn Primary School honours her name, whilst giving pupils the opportunity of aspiring to the company of earlier award-winning scholars.

Now, more than a century since her passing, here is an account of Sarah Jane's life and the world that she once knew. It is the touching story of a teacher's selfless devotion to her pupil and a school's lasting love and respect for its former mistress.

A Village Welcome awaits Sarah Jane

SARAH JANE HOWELL was born on Saturday January 4th 1890 at Abergarw farm in the quiet country setting of Brynmenyn four miles north of Bridgend. She was the daughter of George Howell, a twenty-seven year old carpenter and journeyman from Rhymney, and Jennet, his wife, who represented the latest generation of Morgan's to occupy this small farm, through which the river Ogmore runs its winding course. George and Jennet were now in their second year of marriage, having met when George, an ambitious young man who had moved into the area, stumbled across Abergarw in search of work.

Jennet, aged twenty-six, was a typical farmer's daughter capable of turning her hand to most work whilst responsible for giving Abergarw the feel of a happy and hearty place to live. As a committed companion and best friend to George, she provided the mellowing influence that lightened his load, consumed as he was in building work, possessed of a natural eye for business which inclined his mind and rule-measure towards the next task in hand. In every respect, Jennet was also a housekeeper for Jenkin, her bachelor brother, a mild-mannered, likeable character of traditional farming stock who loved his animals and was never far away from the home fields – although needing Jennet to keep him fed and cared for and on the straight and narrow of life's bumpy course.

Jennet's father, Evan, also lived on the farm, where he was born and bred way back in 1821. He was a man who liked to reminisce about boyhood days, before getting up and stretching his legs in order to see the heifers and calves. He remembered the Royal Mail coach passing through Bridgend, driven by the finest, fastest horses; and the days of the Turnpike trusts, when toll fees were collected on the highways. As a young man he witnessed horse-drawn trams, before trains chugged their way into this quiet corner of Glamorgan as the great invention of the day. But his best stories involved the Llangeinor Arms, a farmers' inn at the top of the nearby mountain, where he joined the local characters for much merriment and a drop to drink, before riding home in his horse-drawn cart down the narrow, bumpy lanes.

Life for Sarah Jane's grandfather had not been without its struggles. He raised his four children, Jennet and Jenkin, as well as Thomas and Catherine, following the loss of his wife, Jane, who met an early end when she failed to recover after falling from a horse. During harsh days of toil and cruel epidemics, Evan kept his family strong and healthy with hard work, which brought food and shelter and peace of mind. But Evan allowed himself time to stop and stare and, as inner contentment seeped into his thoughts, he often amused himself when recalling the enigmatic chapel ministers of his youth. Following family traditions Evan introduced his children to Betharan, a Welsh Congregational Chapel which was the hub and heartbeat of the village, and a discipline throughout life. With Catherine married in the locality and now the birth of Sarah Jane, Evan was a contented man, despite his son, Thomas, having set sail for new horizons, in Ohio, America, where he had settled and would stay.

Evan's thrill was to see Jenkin, his second son, following closely in his footsteps, so that the two shared a vision for the farm besides being friends. In truth, Jenkin devoted himself to Abergarw (meaning the mouth of the river Garw) and ran it in almost every respect, before disappearing to enjoy a drink. When his day's work was done, having cared for the animals as the good shepherd of his pastures, he had removed his muddiest clothes and was on his way. The Miller's Arms was a small thatch-roofed inn situated just a step away near the hump-back bridge of the river Ogmore. Looking out onto the greenery of small paddocks in the distant hills, it shared the soothing sound of fresh water-flow with the old corn mill next door. Despite the presence of nearby quarries and mines, Brynmenyn was a peaceful, even sleepy, little place of small cottages and family-run farms. But Sarah Jane's uncle wished for nowhere else, and here, in his favourite watering-hole, he enjoyed sipping ale with his farming friends.

At this time in Brynmenyn's history, the essential gains of early quarrying gave work to the local men besides defining the village, 'Brynmeinin,' as it used to be known (a hill of stones) – before giving way to today's 'Brynmenyn' (a butter hill). But whatever description is deemed most appropriate, the village had the homely feel of a backwater retreat, broken by the huffing and puffing of friendly trains that chugged their way into the small, but well-kept railway station. Bursting with activity – of lad porters and maintenance men on duty, and a station master whose whistle, loud and shrill, carried a respected blast – it is here that the steam engines were directed either up the nearby Garw or Ogmore valleys. There lay the rich coal seams that fanned the flames of industry and sent trains laden with freight through Brynmenyn, a village that was something of a haven amongst rich mining belts almost all around.

Alongside the railway station, stood the Fox and Hounds Hotel, a big block of a building, tall, sturdy and spacious, peering down from its upstairs rooms almost on top of the moving carriages. This is where beers and spirits were sold to the men of the neighbourhood and community meetings were held in the rooms adjoining the bars, whilst open fires and fine brews offered a warm glow to travellers staying overnight. The Fox and Hounds also shared Sunday services with Betharan Chapel, its next door neighbour; and the good times of weddings and parish teas, besides the sadness and loss when loved ones left the scene and villagers turned-out in great numbers to pay their respects.

Only a few days before Sarah Jane's birth, this same building experienced the unrestrained joy of New Year's Eve: its bars bursting with merrymaking and laughter and muffled mouth organ sounds, not half a mile from the family farm. The Miller's Arms was no different, stocked with casks of beer from Abergarw's own brewery whose malt and hops produced the most agreeable mixtures and were delivered by horse and cart in wooden barrels, usually one at a time.

At such a night as this, taverns were crowded everywhere, all eagerly awaiting the visiting 'Mari Lwyd' revellers who, in accordance with Glamorgan's celebrated customs, arrived on the doorsteps of homes, farms and inns with a rather frightening horse's skull, draped in white sheets and jingling bells. They sung and entertained the crowds, the horse's jaw opening and closing to the sound of each verse, amidst the hilarity and hwyl (good humour) of the occasion. Accepting, with gratitude, the mulled wine and drinks on offer, as well as any loose change donated towards voluntary organisations, the visitors invited locals to match, or to better, their act – whilst others looked on, enjoying the entertainment, merrily drinking the last of the Christmas cheer. Beer measures were poured from large jugs, the white froth floating on top – and, when everyone welcomed the New Year with hymns and arias, most had usually had their fill.

George and Jennet would have heard the distant echoes of exuberance as the men wandered home in the dark early hours – Jenkin, happily amongst them – directed by the faint and flickering glow of dim street lighting. They knew that there was no room for life's hardships on such a night – as laborious work, long hours and little pay paled into insignificance, as did sicknesses, everyday accidents and cold, often damp, conditions at home. George and Jennet wished them well, pleasantly uplifted by their rejoicings, knowing that a difficult year lay ahead for all, in a harsh world where poverty and struggles dominated day to day life.

In truth, men laboured for little reward, digging for valuable minerals, or seeing the food harvests safely home from the open fields. They counted their blessings for the rich natural resources, shaping-up to life's real battles, often hanging-on by their fingertips, hoping, praying and believing that better days lay ahead. Dignity and honour counted greatly and came the way of those who earned their crust from the sweat of their brow. At such times when tramps and vagrants lived roughly in barns and outbuildings, clinging to their freedom and pride, no one could afford to ease up, those failing to sustain themselves suffering the stigma, humiliation and degradation of life in the local workhouse at Bridgend.

George and Jennet took heart in knowing that conditions within this strict, prison-like institution for the homeless, had improved but, equally, they pondered over the ways of a difficult world into which Sarah Jane was to be born. It was a world that relied on the charity and generosity of citizens who had something to spare. Those born into privilege led the way, taking their reward from knowing that it was in the 'giving' that they 'received.' Parcels of land were released for buildings, supplies of stone were offered by quarry owners, and labour was volunteered – with the result that churches, chapels, schools and halls later took their rightful place in society.

Giving and sharing was the order of the day: the Mari Lwyd collections, mentioned earlier, supporting organisations such as the cottage hospital near Bridgend railway station, just as the Salvation Army's deeds were delivered with Christian fellowship in mind. Likewise, when people could not pay medical fees or settle in kind, doctors often chose not to charge, turning a blind eye to their costs or adding them to the bills of wealthier patients who were known to oblige.

It is in the midst of these daily battles that a new generation was arriving onto the scene, Sarah Jane among them, each little soul a living hope for a more promising future, God's way of advancing the world, taking life onward. Within a few years of her birth, Sarah Jane was among the infants of the neighbourhood, arriving on doorsteps standing on her own two feet, singing a verse or rhyme in exchange for a small, but customary gift during this Yuletide season. Wearing a bonnet to keep her head warm and carrying in her small hands a decoration, this gesture, known as 'Y Calennig,' was another Glamorgan custom to celebrate the New Year morn. It was also one that put a toffee or a piece of fruit, or a few nuts into her excited, eager hands, before coming to an abrupt and rather unwelcome end when the clock struck midday.

Family Life at Abergarw Farm

SARAH JANE GREW to enjoy country life amongst all kinds of animals from an early age. Abergarw, a typical modest farm of the day, compensated for its lack of size by way of activity, with cattle, sheep, pigs, horses and poultry of all kinds playing their part, as well as the growing of potatoes, vegetables and some hay and grain. Such was the nature of the day's smaller holdings, and so productive, yet all of these amounted to only a part of old-time farming's cycle of reproduction that saw waste fed back into the soil, making it fertile for future growth. For Sarah Jane, the lambing season brought great interest. At a time when green shoots and buds coloured the hedgerows and heathers, it was a joy to see these four-legged friends bouncing around in a seemingly endless world of play.

At a young age, Sarah Jane, like most farmers' daughters, played her part in the hen-house activities, which involved searching for eggs before jumping aboard the open cart with her mother or uncle to make deliveries. These comical birds, which move around with deliberate steps and scrape the earth for grubs, brought much amusement at feeding time, racing forward in one mad dash, often airborne, to avoid missing out. And when the egg basket started to fill, it meant another journey for Sarah Jane. More importantly, when returning from the local markets, she had usually gained a small coin to save or spend.

The harvesting of fruit and nuts also brought rewards for a growing child whose personality blossomed on the hillside slopes of her native farm. But it was whilst enjoying the attention of her family that another event gave her young existence greater meaning: this being the birth of her sister, Katie, in 1893. Little kept the two apart, Sarah Jane attending to her needs and enjoying the privileges that came with being an elder sibling. Seeing Katie grow from a baby chuckling, cheerfully in her cot, to a not so tiny toddler, filled Sarah Jane with duty and pride, as Katie's daughter, today's Janet Moody, explains:

> When my mother was born, Sarah Jane's world changed completely. She was no longer the smallest in the household and she developed protective instincts of her own. As a caring person, this is where it all began; it was the start of the road for her. The two girls were always close and, living on the farm, the fields became their playground. From day-one they both enjoyed nature, especially herbs and flowers. Michaelmas daisies and cowslips and all the usual flowers were growing on the bank outside the farmhouse.
>
> They were both attracted to the colour and little stopped them from tearing the flowers' heads from the top of their stems. This was as much as they could manage with their small fingers, of course, and, from all accounts, they did a good job of depleting the front garden of much colour. But their love of flowers became more purposeful in later years. They were forever making floral arrangements, putting them into pots and jugs to decorate the house.

From those early days, the two infants shared all they possessed: from secrets and stories to clothes, books, everything, as Janet recalls:

> They had to; nothing went to waste. They also slept in the same bedroom. When I look at old pictures of the farmhouse, it was a long, white-washed building, but it was also narrow. There was not a lot of room, especially when the family grew bigger.
>
> There was a wide gate leading into the yard and then a couple of steps went down to the dwelling. As far as I could see it was more-or-less joined to the barn as one structure. The fields went back to the high levels behind these buildings, into the distance. The village was full of small farms, dozens of them, dotted everywhere. The fields were often no bigger than little paddocks and each holding was self-sufficient.
>
> During wet weather, the Ogmore river which ran through Abergarw's lower fields became fast-flowing and deep, but the girls knew of its dangers. Besides, the river wasn't that inviting for them because this is where the cattle went for water, at least twice a day at the end of milking. Half the time the small herd stood right in the middle of it; so the river was muddy and murky, not the best of places to play.

All the family were thrilled to see Sarah Jane and Katie playing with their cousins when they arrived from Bettws, only a few miles away into the countryside. The farm was a place of great activity and, oftentimes, neighbours called for a jug of milk or for a few eggs, as was accepted and so typical at the time. It was a case of share and share alike. If there were blackberries or hazelnuts to be picked, they would not remain in the hedges for long; they were soon gathered-in and enjoyed by everyone. Likewise, apples and seasonal fruits provided a feast for all, and this was to be expected when villagers helped to bring the hay harvest and other crops from the ripened fields.

With responsibility for the animals and crops, Sarah Jane's uncle, Jenkin, spent most of his time on the farm, and such was his laid-back manner that he was never in too much of a hurry. Janet explains the importance of Jenkin to his young nieces:

> He was the mainstay of the family. Every other word [from the girls' mouths] was 'Jenkin.' He was their favourite person and they looked up to him. He'd take them round the farm and he'd persuade them to help: carrying feed, filling the water buckets, anything that they might enjoy whilst also making his own life easier.'

Not surprisingly, Jenkin's nature instilled confidence and this was to the great benefit of his nieces. They shared a lot of fun, especially as Jennet could be strict and George was often away from Abergarw at work. But neither parent failed to give their fullest personal attention to their daughters, as Janet knows well:

> Correcting the children was left to their mother, who was known as Mumma. She was the disciplinarian. But I also know that their father, Duda, treated them in an adult way. He'd spend time sitting and reading with them, taking them aside. He was the one who passed on information, and education meant everything to him.'

It was their mother, however, who showed them how to bake tarts and knead the dough, resulting in the aroma of freshly-baked bread, which emerged from the fireside oven, built into the thick stone walls of the hearth. Preparing pots of broth, known as cawl, was another task: a regular and solid meal in the winter months, full of vegetables, onions and chunks of fatty meat. This is what kept the cold weather at bay, also silencing uncle Jenkin and his helpers when they arrived on the pantry doorstep at lunchtime.

Severe winters came with the need to chop potatoes and turnips for the cattle, just as the boiling of vegetable-peelings fed the pigs. These amusing animals with floppy ears and studious expressions ate whatever landed in their troughs, causing their weight to teeter around the twenty-score mark, a considerable weight, when killed and salted during the colder months. This is when Jenkin separated the joints, dividing all amongst local farmers who returned the compliment when their own swine went, in turn, the same way – so that pieces hung by skewered hooks from the dairy beams, one flitch besides another, mostly a mass of fat, broken by lean bacon streaks few and far between. Nevertheless, when important visitors such as the doctor or minister called, Jennet took delight in wrapping-up a few pieces as a treat for them to take home.

During these days of Sarah Jane's early childhood, there were casual workers helping on the Brynmenyn farms. Many were from Ireland, men who had in earlier years settled in the area following the potato famine in their native land. And there was the regular arrival and departure of travelling merchants, some of whom lodged on the farm. Janet continues:

> I have a census confirming that a man from Carmarthen was staying overnight around the 1890s. He is described as a clothier and came round selling his wares. The family would buy reams of materials from him, because sheets, underwear and most items were handmade. According to my mother, these traders would stay a week or so, exploring the area, looking for business before moving on.

Cattle and fat stock marts at Bridgend, Cowbridge and Llantwit Major were now big events, as were the sheep sales, where farmers and herdsmen directed the animals down winding lanes, often for many miles in all kinds of weather. Horse-drawn carts followed behind, bulging with homemade products such as baskets and blankets as farmworkers and country folk enjoyed their time together. And once the auctioneer's hammer had determined the destiny of the fat stock, there was time enough for a drink and fireside fellowship before the journey home.

This is where Jennet was hard at work: cleaning the farmhouse from the mud of dirty boots, arranging the grate, tending to the fires, dusting the furniture. Her tasks were never-ending as her niece, Janet, explains:

> They had an old sideboard and rather a lot of china ornaments. Mumma was never idle and as soon as Sarah Jane was old enough she had her little jobs. Washing clothes by hand was a regular task. This was before they had a scrubbing board, when they used an old 'dolly.' I know this because it has since been given to me. It

consists of a round copper object, which is attached to a long pole. They used to beat the clothes with this to remove the mud. Tubs of water were filled up in the dairy and they'd have some form of clothes line attached to the farmhouse. I imagine it to be an old rope propped up by a piece of wood. Uncle Jenkin was the practical one; he'd have arranged this.

The simple ways of life carried the day, yet no one could deny that farming had by now progressed steadily as modern practices, having survived strict scrutiny, were put in place. In *The Glamorgan Gazette*, regular advertisements offered the latest in chaff cutters, mowers, reapers, sheep racks and feeding troughs. Likewise, in the nearby market town of Cowbridge, the 'Eagle, Corn, Seed, Manure and Implements Store' was in demand, firmly at the forefront of every farmer's mind – as were the private loans, from as little as £3 and upwards, which tempted landowners such as Jenkin to spend. Progress had been steady and sure, rather like the farm horses: respected for their part in turning the wheels of agriculture and everyday life, uncomplainingly, for as far back as people could recall.

At home in Abergarw, Sarah Jane saw the horses as being an extension to the family, and their doleful-look and loyal, hardworking nature made them much-loved. Her uncle, Jenkin, treated them as his trustworthy friends, ensuring they were well fed, watered and rested; regularly taken to farriers to be shoed; given bedding in their stables, and pampered with carrots and other treats. In return, they tackled all manner of work: transporting manure onto the land; dragging cutters and cultivators across the fields, and pulling cart-loads of produce into the stores. In fairness, they also knew the way home late at night, when their owners were too sleepy, or merry, to take to the reins.

In every respect, horses led the way and little moved without them. They featured at the annual Glamorganshire Ploughing Match at nearby Cowbridge and at the Vale of Glamorgan Agricultural Show – whilst at St Mary Hill, between Bridgend and Cowbridge, they provided every reason for one of the biggest fairs in the country. Each year, August 26th was a day to look forward to when horse dealers and traders arrived from far away, before having to climb narrow, twisting country lanes to an isolated mountain top location. It was there on a plateau-like summit overlooking Bridgend and distant counties – even beyond the Bristol Channel as far as Exmoor's *Lorna Doone* moorlands – that deals were made amongst the excitement of an action packed day. Tom Harry, who has lived his life near this famous old venue, and whose father remembers the fair during Sarah Jane's lifetime, has this to say:

> St Mary Hill Fair was noted throughout Britain; it was the biggest horse fair of its kind and brought people in from everywhere, many from Ireland. They would arrive a week early, setting up camp, lighting fires and pitching tents on every spare patch of grass around the mountain. Twelve acres were set aside by the Radcliffe Estate and the entire area was packed on the big day. Besides serving the farming community, the fair was a

special occasion for everyone. Horses were so important then and dealers were present from everywhere; they were all influential, big employers, often distinguished with long black frock-coats and bowler hats.

Tom is aware of a plaque, donated by Bernard Battrick from nearby Llangan, standing at the site of the old fairground, stating that the event originated way back in the fifteenth century. And, come what may, everybody arrived at this unique setting to enjoy themselves, despite commotion and controversy often forcing a way onto the scene. Police constables were known to be busy and fights would break out although most came and went without major disturbances. No one could forget these events, least of all Tom:

> Any grudges were settled there and then, often in the middle of a tight circle of onlookers who converged – as a human wall – around those involved. In later years cattle were also sold [adding more chaos to the day]. They'd arrive in rail trucks at Bridgend station and they'd be herded to the fairground. They'd pass along the same cluttered little lanes as the mares and ponies, which were tied head-to-tail by rope and halters to a leading horse. And there were steam engines, food carts, beer wagons and pedestrians everywhere.

Understandably, the activities of this bumper day in August filled large columns in the local newspapers. *The Glamorgan Gazette* of April 29th 1890 stated that to be absent for St Mary Hill Fair 'would be to some people a never failing source of regret, a calamity in their brief existence.' Stating that it captured the interest of 'old and young alike,' the paper added that there are individuals who 'boast of having been present at every St Mary Hill Fair for the last fifty years'... but would Sarah Jane have been amongst the masses when she grew old enough, one wonders? Well, yes, Tom seems to think so:

> It was a special day for all the family, for everyone; and people would dress up to go. They arrived to enjoy themselves. There'd be marquees and refreshments and food and beer; and sales of saddles and carts. There were boxing booths, and Freeman's side-stalls and fairground attractions. Farm workers gathered in their droves, some found future work there, and they'd mix with the coal miners who didn't want to miss the day. They were there in great numbers, having booked a day's leave well in advance – many of them having jumped on to the back of a mare for a free ride to the ground.

All of this happened on a remote mountain-top where, in addition to the liquor tents, there were two special hostelries situated nearby. One was 'The Bell', a few hundred yards away from the fairground on the road returning to Bridgend, where the church yard next door provided rest for those who drunk themselves to sleep – whilst in the opposite direction, and a similar distance from the big event, 'Yr Hen Dafarn' (The Old Pub) catered for the crowds returning homewards towards Llantrisant. Both inns enjoyed a bumper trade during the week of the fair –

before the gatherings dispersed and life returned to its normal and more orderly pace.

It was in a similar fashion, slow, steady and unhurried, that the days moved along at Abergarw, where Sarah Jane knew the meaning of hard work and being busy whilst seizing happiness along the way. Then, as in all households, when the busy week was over, Sunday became a celebrated day of rest. Lunch with vegetables and meat – both having been prepared the previous evening – were followed by a pudding, usually of fruits in a pastry tart, as formality and religion dictated the order of the day.

From a young age Sarah Jane was taken to Betharan Chapel, one of the oldest and most respected buildings in the village where, in Sunday school, she made friends as the seeds of later worship were sown. She, like members of her family, looked forward to this day, when black suits and hats were worn by men and mantle cloaks, capes and costumes by the Victorian women, with eye-catching bonnets and accessories. In time, Sarah Jane was introduced to Bible stories and readings and, from these early years, her disciplined and faithful behaviour was set in stone for life.

Childhood Days amongst the
Mines and Minerals

B RYNMENYN HAD EXISTED in the midst of mining work for generations before Sarah Jane's birth and her forefathers would have experienced the modest early diggings that took place around Abergarw farm. Grandfather Evan had personally witnessed this activity in the nearby valleys and in neighbouring Aberkenfig, Bryncethin and Tondu, and he knew about the trials and tribulations that the good and honest miners faced in their quest for a living. Indeed, meeting the demands of iron ore and coal had long since put South Wales on the map, and Brynmenyn and district fully played its part.

At the railway station, a short walk away from the farm buildings, no one could miss miners, young and old, passing through the village and returning homewards, tired and weary, black with dust and grime. In earlier days, mining had seen innocent youngsters pulling small trolley 'boxes' underground and although such child labour had now ended, the work carried out was severely challenging, physically gruelling, mentally wearisome and fraught with danger to life and health. Only a mile or two from Brynmenyn, the late David Bayliss, born in 1877, left the following reminder of how things once were:[1]

---

[1] An interview by Leonard Higgins, July 15th 1954 - *The Higgins Papers*: Bridgend Library Services.

Between 1830 and 1840, a man named Robert Watson from Cowbridge had several small *sinkings* on the mountain at Bryncethin, and they were known to us from childhood as Robert Watson's Pits. He used to come and pay his workmen at the old Corner House [inn], opposite the new Mason's Arms.[2]

Before this, John Bedford, from Birmingham, had his own coal and iron ore industry at Cefn Cribwr, nearby, complete with brickworks and forge. He created jobs for the men, just as Sir Robert Price and John Brogden had done in later years – when a young Evan Morgan, harrowing clods of earth in the Abergarw fields, would have seen in the distant hills the smoke of foundries and chimneys escaping into the countryside air. Such industrialists breathed life and influence into the community and Mr Brogden's family is noted for helping Porthcawl's rise to a 19th century port with new harbour and enhanced railway links to Maesteg in the Llynfi Valley.[3]

Sarah Jane's family recognised the toil and tears that went into digging the *black diamond*, as coal was often referred to, especially the shining, hard-burning, anthracite. There were open cast mines nearer the surface and deeper pits sunk into the lower-lying seams, and many appeared as a cluster of stone buildings, set against isolated, bleak backgrounds. There were out-houses,

[2] *Bryncethin* by David Bayliss (within *The Higgins Papers*):
    Bridgend Library Services.
[3] *Pioneers of the Welsh Coalfields,* Elizabeth Phillips, the *Western Mail* 1925
    Chapter XXVIII 'First Developments in Mid Glamorgan,'
    (within *The Higgins Papers*): Bridgend Library Services.

stables and engine sheds; pulley wheels and furnaces, whilst dangerous-looking equipment like traction engines heaped soil into man-made mounds. Nearby, railway wagons were piled high with stock as crowds of men, pit-ponies and harnessed-horses sucked in the fresh air before returning underground.

Amongst the men on the scene – and these included blacksmiths, carters, sawyers, drivers, hostlers, stablemen and many more – the pit proprietors and colliery agents were immensely important, carrying big responsibilities and usually living in fine residences near the works. Of course, they presided over pockets of mass activity, energy and danger, which were the lifeblood of the valleys, and they were known to all. Colliery officials provided wages, security and often housing, besides putting bread regularly onto the table of miners' wives, children and relatives.

Understandably, such senior officials were well looked-after. Their families were helped with household chores by the colliers, so that fires, for instance, would be fully alight and glowing and warming living rooms by the time everyone went downstairs for breakfast. Katie, Sarah Jane's sister, witnessed this at first-hand whilst visiting the daughter of a colliery agent living in one of the adjacent valleys and her sense of surprise is today shared by Katie's own daughter, Janet:

> The two had met in school and had become friendly.
> Occasionally my mother slept the night at her home and
> she was amazed how much the miners did for the
> family. No job was too much trouble and this was a

reflection of how important the girl's father was. My mother was shocked to learn that if, for instance, she left her shoes outside the bedroom door, they would be clean and polished and shining by the time she dressed next morning. Being used to doing things for herself, this was an experience that she never forgot.

Everyone at home in Abergarw was brought up to respect the miners. Our family were farmers, forever busy on the land, with no relatives or connections in the mines at all; but everyone knew of the dangers underground and kept away. Before my mother was born – when Sarah Jane was a two-year-old – there was an explosion in Aberkenfig, near Tondu, on Brynmenyn's doorstep. In later years I came across this old, disused mine when cutting across the fields towards Cefn Cribwr. I remember the open expanse and the ground underfoot being bumpy and overgrown with grass, and realising that during its former days this is where so many people had lost their lives.

Janet was referring to the Parc Slip colliery that experienced a disaster in 1892, the most awful reminder to local inhabitants of how severe mining accidents can be – and despite men emerging from the scene alive, having earlier been feared dead, the heavy death toll was more than the hard-working community could bear. The Bryncethin School Log Book[4] recorded this never-to-be-forgotten incident, and the loss and heartbreak for pupils and their families is hard to imagine.

---

[4]   Details are found in *The Higgins Papers*: Bridgend Library Services.

August 26th 1892… A terrible explosion took place this morning in the neighbourhood; few children came to school.

Frank John, one of the fortunate men to be rescued was aware that this catastrophe took place on the day of St Mary Hill Fair when scores of miners had taken leave to attend the event and, ultimately, this was to spare their lives. This gentleman recorded his memories of the tragedy in a touching poem, *Parc Slip Explosion 1892*, a copy of which is held at Bridgend Reference Library in both Welsh and English. Here are some of the sad, telling verses which follow the introductory lines:

> Amongst the dead and wounded
> It was an awful sight,
> To fight the poisonous gases
> From morning until night.

> No sign of no-one coming
> Our hearts were in a gloom,
> Patiently awaiting
> Down in a living tomb.

> About one o'clock in the morning,
> Here came the 'After Damp'
> When we were almost in darkness
> With the aid of only one lamp.

> We prayed on the Lord Almighty
> To save us from this death,
> When we could hear some of our comrades
> Breathing their last breath.

Now all young men take warning,
In life make no delay.
Be ready night and morning
For no-one knows his dying day.

Such events galvanised the pit proprietors and the country's leaders to aspire to ever-higher standards of safety. Various acts brought direct intervention into the mines, with important officials often sleeping overnight at Brynmenyn's Fox and Hounds Hotel on their way to making pit inspections. These measures and the beginning and growth of mining federations were a sign of the future that were all so reassuring to housewives and parents living in constant fear for their loved ones underground. But, disputes on pay and safety would long continue, and led to demonstrations which, sometimes, disturbed the gentle peace on the village green near Betharan Chapel. On April 22nd 1898, when Sarah Jane was aged eight, *The Glamorgan Gazette* shared this news about Brynmenyn:

The Strike

Several colliery horses have passed through our village this last week. It seems as if the miners' strike is going to last for a time. It is to be hoped that a settlement will soon be arrived at.

With sustained coal output flourishing in the three valleys that converged on Brynmenyn – the Ogmore, Garw and Llynfi – steam trains pulled coal wagons through the landscape all day long, as Sarah Jane's niece, Janet again explains:

Most of the men living in our village were, in fact, railwaymen and many more were to move into the district from Somerset. Down the road, Tondu was extremely busy; there were gangs of men running the trains, tending to the lines, working the depots. Every day the family at Abergarw saw the trucks going past; the rail track was close to the farmyard. They'd have been empty or carrying wood [for pit props] on their way up [the valley], and full of coal coming back down.

Understandably, when the day's work was done and the men whistled their way home, there was much happiness and relief. And such times were meant for sharing: home life, with the family; company, with friends; the inn fireside, with the locals, and the ale, with fellow-drinkers. The day's duties amounted to thirsty work and it was expected that the beer flowed: regulars retiring to a nearby bush, or behind a big tree, discreetly, as a matter of personal convenience. Breweries were profitable businesses: Abergarw's being just a minute's walk from the farmhouse on the site of the old corn and woollen mills, where the Howell family noticed horse and carts taking away and returning heavy wooden beer barrels and casks, just as the trains would come and go. Well known in the district, Abergarw Brewery advertised in style and the following is a typical entry that appeared in *The Glamorgan Gazette* in the 1890s:

Abergarw Golden Bitter Ale
Brewed from the Choicest Hops and Best Malt
1s 2d per gallon – Sold in 9, 12, 18 gallon casks.

'And now sending this ale out in brilliant condition.
It is a healthy, delightful beverage,
and a splendid tonic for the system.'
John Brothers, Abergarw Brewery, near Bridgend.

This family concern stood tall, as a beacon, and was respected throughout the district during Sarah Jane's lifetime. One of its shareholders was George Howell, her father, who, being almost a teetotaller was far from the brewery's best customer. However, George was known to support sales and a half-pint stone bottle of his, still unopened, is in the possession of the family today. It bears the brewery address as Abergarw, '*near Brynmenyn,*' proving just how proud a hamlet in its own right Abergarw once was.

The brewery served inn keepers for miles around, its thirst-quenching ales fuelling the social scene. Only a punt away from Abergarw's lower fields, rugby football had become well established with Bryncethin's side a match for the local teams. This was hardly surprising with miners, rock hard and bursting to run around in the fresh air, competing for ball and bragging-rights in the packed enclosures of fierce rivalry. Success on the field set the men apart, elevating the most talented to heroic heights, before leading to sing-songs and happy bar scenes when the day's battles were done.

But it was the rousing choral performances and male voice concerts that lifted the spirits of the Howell family, as well as cantatas and operas that were staged courtesy of local artists. These were held in community halls, churches and chapels, whilst Bachelor Balls, Railway Servants'

Dinners and children's pantomimes were frequently taking place. Up the road in Blaengarw Workmen's Hall, Ivor Novello, Cardiff's famous composer, once entertained, whilst on the bigger stage, Bridgend Town Hall, a towering landmark with stately columns, steps and eye-catching advertisement boards offered varied programmes to match the sense of occasion that lay beyond its big front doors. The Gwyn Hall in Neath was another, a train ride away, where Adelina Patti, the well-known soprano singer and a charitable woman, was raising money for the poor.

By coincidence, this much-travelled and many-times-married celebrity, who thrilled audiences in faraway parts, was often seen taking tea at the Miller's Arms in Brynmenyn. It was in the parlour of this popular little public house, where next door the men – including Uncle Jenkin – tapped the tables with earthenware pots for more beer, that she struck-up a friendship with Mrs Jones, the owner. Known as 'Kitty Abergarw,' this lady is said to have used china from her best tea set – previously left undisturbed in a corner cabinet since Kitty's wedding day – as a mark of respect, although being totally unaware of her visitor's identity and fame.[5] Janet Moody is aware of these visits:

> My mother used to see Adelina Patti from the farm across the road. And from all accounts she liked something stronger to drink as well as a cup of tea! She had friends in Waterton and often visited the Miller's Arms, but in those

---

[5]   *The Glamorgan Gazette,* of July 15th 1976: Bridgend Library Services.

days she was not so well recognised. Nowadays, she'd have been a big celebrity; her face appearing on front covers, in magazines, there for all to see.

Of course, singing and music, often in the churches and chapels, was the best entertainment going. Talent was nurtured from an early age in Sunday school. Children spent time practising, rehearsing and learning their lines, until they became good at what they were doing. My mother and Sarah Jane enjoyed the piano; they were keen and had lessons. They worked hard and wanted to progress and they pushed each other in this respect.

And they were seldom apart; they enjoyed each other's company. Sometimes, they'd wander up to the woods for some fresh air and a natter; they liked a bit of gossip as girls do. Then they used to play tennis. There was a court alongside the Miller's Arms, near the old waterwheel. They'd relax there, hitting the ball about – neither of them any good, I don't suppose – but they'd have looked the part in their long dresses and respectable white shades. Life was a lot more innocent then; people made their own fun. Well, they had to, of course, especially in a quiet place like Brynmenyn.

At home the story was much the same; Janet continues:

Everybody was happy doing their own things. Young girls like Sarah Jane would be good at sewing, darning, knitting and tapestry. They liked to be useful and were creative around the house. Men also had their own jobs and hobbies and favourite things to do and everybody mucked in. By now many [people] had bicycles and cycling clubs were established and going strong. There'd be races from time to time, usually over short distances of perhaps two or three miles, and these were a real novelty, drawing the crowds, and they were greatly enjoyed. There'd also be trips down to the beach and to flower shows and fetes. On the farm, neighbours used to call. They spent the evening playing games and, perhaps, singing around the piano. Someone might arrive with a flute or another instrument. It was all pretty ordinary but this is how life ticked along.

Janet's words mirror the message of an unidentified poem, today held in Brynmenyn Primary School entitled *The Good Old Days,* which describes the childhood era enjoyed by Sarah Jane. The verses speak of 'no vandals, no muggings' for 'there was [little] to rob,' at a time when people were rich 'with just a couple of bob.' It was an age when home fires burnt brightly and no one 'locked [their] doors;' when 'there was no holiday abroad' or 'carpets on floors.' And, as the poem draws to a close, the reassuring words confirm that despite the simplicity of life and all its limitations and concerns, people were 'happier in those far off days.' They were also 'kinder and caring in so many ways.'

Schooling at Bryncethin

A S A CHILD, Sarah Jane benefited from the compulsory education that was introduced during the reign of Queen Victoria. This had been a slow and difficult process whereby old ways and habits, often defended to the last, were replaced so that legislation could shape a more promising future. Indeed, in 1891, the year that followed Sarah Jane's birth, the weekly *School Pence Fees* that had hitherto been levied, were also lifted, meaning that primary education for children became free.

This good news arrived at a time when board schools benefited from the work of conscientious managers who felt the honour and thrill of being elected to their posts. Progress was encouraging although it did not stop a number of parents keeping their children at home, working the farms and doing jobs deemed more important. Likewise, others were opposed to the indoctrination that swayed attitudes and preferences within the classrooms, usually born of religion, and neither would they budge. Such varying opinions made for compelling battles although education won the day as an investment that would lead the country to enterprise and prosperity in later years.

Sarah Jane's family had lived through these challenging times and each member had his or her own experiences to recall. Grandfather Evan arrived on the scene too early for classroom work, but he counted his blessings in being able to step into the green fields with his sickle and scythe. As a farmer, he was doing all that he knew and wanted to do: caring for his animals in the fresh country air, and this would not change. All four of his children also missed the full benefits of a formal education, although each had gained from Sunday school at Betharan. And, whilst the boys, Thomas and Jenkin, took to the fields, squaring-up to the rigours of farm work – Catherine and Jennet were busily involved with domestic duties. They revelled in most housework, just like other girls of their age who were adept at cleaning, cookery, culinary, and all the rest.

George Howell likewise was raised a little early for compulsory lessons and in the absence of tuition he rolled-up his sleeves and taught himself. George liked to break problems down into smaller parts just as his father, a wise and knowing blacksmith, had done in his native Rhymney valley. George realised that, fundamentally, learning required an enquiring mind and a desire to gain knowledge. With these both in his grasp, he went on his way, advancing from a junior carpenter who once journeyed from village to village in search of work, to becoming an influential figure in this important trade. Wood, a natural material, was used to make many essential day-to-day requirements; and, mastery of the carpentry craft, coupled with dexterity with a dowel in hand, gave him a lifetime of gainful employment. Short in stature he may well have been but, in aspirations, he stood tall, becoming a clerk to the local works and being admired for the design of houses that he was to build.

George paddled his own canoe, working steadily for gains that came later in life.

Both George and Jennet realised that the beginning of schooling in Bryncethin, just a mile and a half up the road from Abergarw farm, reflected the contributions made by church and chapels within local parishes. This early-day Infants school, which is understood to have been in existence in 1870 and which benefited from the legacy of an elderly lady who bequeathed her cottage to the church to provide lessons,[6] was now a convenient place of learning under the watchful eyes of diocese members who managed and monitored its progress. Their regular visits brought detailed reports that usually leaned towards the Bible, as the school Log Book[7] entry of October 26th 1898 implies:

> Throughout the department, and especially in the lower divisions, a further syllabus of Religious Instruction should be given. In particular the New Testament is inadequate, and private Prayers (morning and evening), should be taught throughout the school.
>
> The answering in Scripture should, as far as possible, be in the exact words of the Bible. Hymns, well-known and in illustrations of the Scripture subject taught, would materially help to make the subjects attractive and interesting.

There was no misunderstanding this message and Sarah Jane, a fluent Welsh speaker, also knew better than to

---

6   *Bryncethin by David Bayliss,* Higgins Papers: Bridgend Library Services.

7   Bryncethin Infants National School Log Book 1884 – 1907: Glamorgan Archive Services.

converse freely in her native tongue during school hours, for this was not allowed. Discipline was strict and she avoided stepping out of line. Children were taught respect in the knowledge that the cane, or a severe reprimand, awaited those who strayed beyond the boundary, whilst a bigger row followed at home. Of course, the *Three R's,* Reading, Writing and Arithmetic led the way, all core subjects that set the platform for later learning, supported by a variety of objective lessons that took place both inside and outside classrooms.

Sarah Jane's sister, Katie, often spoke about her days at this same church school in Bryncethin, which was an old building situated near the junction that joined Wigan and Ogmore Terraces. Katie used to step out of Abergarw farm, through the gate and up the road. It was a hilly climb but everyone was used to walking and, at least, it gave her time to prepare for what lay ahead, as her daughter, Janet, explains today:

> What I know about my mother also applies to Sarah Jane because there was little between their ages and they were similar girls. At the time the church school in Bryncethin was the only place for them to go; there was nowhere else and they had to get on with it. They had to walk along a narrow road but it was pretty safe. There were no cars or pavements then, only bicycles and carts. I'd imagine there'd have been one or two other children keeping them company. And, they didn't loll about; they had to get there on time, or else there'd be trouble when they arrived.

Even during *my* schooldays discipline was strict, so we can imagine how harsh punishment was in earlier times. It didn't take much to bring out the cane. On one occasion, my mother was reprimanded for speaking Welsh. She happened to be playing in the school yard when she was caught and she never forgot this or the humiliation of having to stand in the corner throughout the next lesson. She thought the teachers were only interested in English – but the experience taught her what was right and wrong, and she didn't repeat the mistake again.

In *The Glamorgan Gazette* regular monthly articles describe the activities of the Llangeinor School Board whose managers were now meeting regularly at the Fox and Hounds Hotel.[8] There, beyond the two well-worn entrance steps of the building, distinguished men of the local valley schools worked through detailed agendas. They reviewed salaries and increments; granted free-time to teachers for scholarship examinations; monitored pupil sickness and truancy, and worked to the recommendations of government inspectors' reports. Above all, they studied absenteeism in detail, ticking-back attendance registers to the list of pupils, painstakingly, to safeguard the continued receipt of financial grants. Filling classrooms mattered greatly and if numbers dropped, excuses were sometimes made to send children home rather than to report low figures. As for persistent offenders, they could expect the

---

[8]   Monthly reports of the Llangeinor School Board in *The Glamorgan Gazette*, one appearing on February 7th 1890: Bridgend Library Services.

visit of a truancy inspector, whose stern punishment would frighten transgressors back into line.

With the opening of Wyndham Board School in Nantymoel and other similar establishments across Glamorgan, locals in Brynmenyn knew that it was only a question of time before the village provided lessons of its own. Education's march forward was gathering pace and, despite staunch dissenters being still less than convinced – and the inevitable absenteeism at times of hay harvests, blackberry-picking and potato weeks – lessons had arrived and would stay. Attitudes were also changing, for many believed that denominational schools no longer offered the best way forward in a changing world as earlier motives and deep-set values were thrown open to discussion and fuller debate.

At a time when Abergarw's Evan and Jenkin and local farmers in Glamorgan were benefiting from the rather different lessons of government-backed butter-making schools – whereby visiting experts conducted classes across England and Wales to pass on best practices to dairymen – more celebrations were taking place at Abergarw because George and Jennet's third daughter, Beatrice, had been born, whilst Margaret, known as Margot, was to follow close behind. With the new additions keeping schooling at the forefront of family minds, the future placement of Sarah Jane at the scene of higher education was also being considered. At a time when Bridgend Boys and Girls Intermediate School had become established and the County High School for Girls at Cowbridge was popular, a number of other suitable venues, such as the Glen View, Port Talbot, were being well-advertised and recommended in national newspapers, and were within comfortable reach by rail.

The reality that George and Jennet had to comprehend, however, was that schooling of a secondary nature was not so actively encouraged for girls, for their roles in life were more readily linked with family duties and supporting a husband. More so, for those who were fortunate to secure good work, such as teaching, there was an alarming pay-differential between male and female employees which tended to discourage girls from stepping onto a career path. If the Abergarw farm daughters intended entering into a profession they would have to compete in a man's world and Sarah Jane, the eldest, needed to prepare herself well, for she would be leading the way.

Grandfather Evan Dies
as a New Century Dawns

SPRING HAD ALWAYS BEEN A FAVOURITE SEASON for Sarah Jane's grandfather, Evan Morgan. It was a time for him to sit up and marvel as a blaze of rich green colours broke onto the farm meadows as far as his eyes could see. Evan acknowledged the mystery of such a transformation, executed to perfection, yet way beyond the control of human hands. Soon the crops and harvest followed, courtesy of more bounteous gifts of nature, filling the pantry floor with food, and the storage sheds with hay and grain. For a farmer who had dedicated a lifetime to the land, the arrival of this special time of year provided an injection of energy and great joy, and this continued into Evan's later life by which time a heart complaint had slowed him down. But by the time Easter approached in 1898, Evan, then in his seventy-seventh year and generally weaker, was to see the last of the spring sunshine, for he died a few days after Palm Sunday on April 14th.

Immediately, Abergarw fell under a big black cloud. Evan had been ever-present on the farm all his life and, although he offered little help during his later years, he was a stable influence and his experience cast a protective net over the household. He was a much-loved family man who had lived his life quietly and without controversy –

although, interestingly, he fell-foul of the law just one day before Sarah Jane was born. He never forgot that first week in January 1890, when Police Constable Vernon reported him because five of his pigs had wandered from the farm onto the public road,[9] and he had to pay a fine of ten shillings in addition to costs. Now his days had ended, and a short obituary in The Glamorgan Gazette on Friday April 22nd 1898 read as follows:

> It is with deep regret that we announce the death of one of our oldest inhabitants, Mr Evan Morgan, Abergarw farm. The funeral took place last Monday at the village chapel, which was well attended.

In an old newspaper cutting from family records dated two weeks later, it states that although Evan had been involved at Betharan Chapel since he was a child, it was only in later years that he had been 'received into the communion of the church.' The article added that Evan 'had the reputation of being a kind neighbour and was of a sociable disposition which, coupled with the fact that he had spent so many years in the same place, made him well known throughout the district.' He had, apparently, been noticed outside Abergarw farmhouse the day before he was called to rest, no doubt wearing a customary white ruff around his lower jaw, which gave his features a softer, angelic look.

---

[9] The Glamorgan Gazette, January 17th 1890: Bridgend Library Services.

George missed Evan greatly, for he had been a wise counsellor and good friend over the years and, besides his many kindnesses, he encouraged and supported George's good intentions, such as the building of a row of three terraced houses across the road from the farm. Each one had been finished well, delighting Evan, whilst representing all that was good about architecture of this age. Now in a world without his father-in-law, George could reflect upon Evan's era, and how life had quietly moved along since he was a boy.

Times were 'darker' then and, besides the hardships of earlier mining, quarrying and long hours of labour, most progress came with a big struggle. However, Evan had taken delight in simple pleasures, like watching his family growing up in front of his eyes and supporting his good intentions for the farm, reaping the rewards of the seeds he had laboriously planted by hand. Understandably, he admired the honest traders of his age, and he enjoyed watching the blacksmiths and wheelwrights coating cartwheels with a hot rim of iron and seeing the metal contracting as it cooled. He had also caught the tail-end of oxen tilling the land, until replaced by the heavy-duty Shire horses and the industrious Welsh cobs, whose bigger feet and greater agility, speed, and spontaneity were to later lead the way.

During Evan's retirement years, he enthralled many with his tales. He had seen houses sprouting up across Abergarw and Llangeinor, and the latest buildings were different from his younger days. He had also been fascinated by Bridgend's growth, admiring modern workmanship, such as the terrace at Park Street that spread so elegantly down the hill. Evan had first-hand knowledge of the floods of 1877, when the river Ogmore spilled into the town and the Wyndham Hotel was six-feet-under.[10] He, like others, felt the shocking force of the rain and storms, sending inhabitants upstairs, as little boats sailed down the streets delivering food supplies and help.

Evan was born only a few years after Queen Victoria and they had seen similar things in life, although from a different perspective. Poverty, sickness, malnutrition, and limited opportunities were obstacles to be overcome, whilst Brougham's coaches and carriages, wind-powered sailing boats and later Penny Farthing bicycles were moving progress. The world was a different place: everybody knew their hamlets, villages and parishes, happily congregating for water at the village well and walking to the food markets and flannel fairs in the neighbourhood, but venturing little further besides.

Evan took stock of the advancements made during Queen Victoria's reign, not only in schooling, but with train locomotives, steam-powered shipping, and a new-age industrial platform. He noted the creativity and design of inspirational engineers of this era, especially Isambard Kingdom Brunel, whose work, such as Temple Meads Railway Station and Clifton Suspension Bridge, had taken engineering to new heights. Likewise, when crowds

---

[10] Periodic reports in *The Glamorgan Gazette* during August 1877: Bridgend Library Services.

flocked to London to share the Queen's *Diamond Jubilee* in 1897, Evan was not far from the crowded scenes at Dunraven Place, where Bridgend's own celebrations of the Queen's remarkable sixty-year reign took place.

Although Evan was saddened to see his son, Thomas, emigrating, this departure strengthened his bond with Jenkin. They shared special moments throughout the years, knuckling-down together with will and determination to move Abergarw forward. From a young age Evan passed his knowledge and skills onto Jenkin, whose own enjoyment of country-life mirrored his father's interests. They also shared the same concerns, such as seeing the rivers of their valleys polluted and discoloured by coal wash and waste – a source of heated discussion at angling dinners and events – although they both understood the broader issues involved. It was not surprising that Jenkin inherited Evan's sharp eye and steady hand for a shotgun and, besides spelling an early end for many a rabbit and pheasant this meant that Jenkin was occasionally called to duty in the neighbourhood when events got out of hand.

On one occasion, which happened to be Evan's last Christmas day in 1897, Jenkin was summoned to Brynmenyn village, where a wild boar attacked a pedestrian. Even in those days the bailiffs and authorities frowned heavily on stray animals, often sheep, pushing their way through hedges onto the highways, which usually resulted in them being rounded up in an enclosure known as 'a pound' at River Row where the payment of a fine by owners secured their release.[11] And there is no doubt that Evan shared with his son the funny side of this, otherwise, serious story about a disruptive and dangerous animal, which was described, light-heartedly, in an article in *The Glamorgan Gazette* of March 4th 1898 entitled a 'Boar's Christmas Outing at Brynmenyn.'

The story describes the attack on poor-old Henry Trott, a gardener who, having been bitten by the animal, could not work for a month. The incident occurred outside the Fox and Hounds where a local minister and his father came to the victim's rescue. Indeed, Thomas Williams, of Brynmenyn, the senior of the two, amused the gathered jury with his excited version of events for he also felt the animal's teeth. He spoke of the 'close shave of losing his [own] leg as the boar went for him,' adding in defence of Trott's sober nature 'there was no taste or smell of any drink [on him].' Overcoming the boar had been a struggle and at the end of the ordeal Mr Trott, battered, bewildered and beaten, asked where he was and 'complained of his leg being hurt.'

We can only imagine the scene at Abergarw farmhouse on this eventful Christmas day: Jennet cooking the joint, George tending to the fires, Sarah Jane playing with her sisters, Evan snoozing in his chair – and Jenkin returning a hero, tipsy from the inevitable celebrations that crowned his conquest, but the same happy, hearty Jenkin, unhurried and relaxed, with his faithful farm dogs close at hand. Evan may

---

[11]   *A Short History of Brynmenyn (1820 – 1900)* by Bill Lavis,
Brynmenyn Primary School records.

have taken Sarah Jane aside, not so much to explain the deed her uncle had performed but to provide a gentle reminder of the unpredictable nature of animals, especially wild boars whose hunger is never to be underestimated. Evan was known to spoil his family with kindnesses and Sarah Jane was a recipient in this same way.

Of course, when the axe fell upon Jenkin to shoot the beast that day, his father could think of no one better to perform the task. Evan was understood to be in good health at this particular time, although his well-being suffered in the months that followed. But he had stayed long enough to see Brynmenyn facing a brighter future. Besides the nearby Iron and Gas works at Tondu and the coke ovens, the local coal trade continued to lead the way and, with news about a new drift mine alongside the village brickworks, the employment scene was encouraging for the local men.

Already electricity was the talk of Bridgend town and, whilst its arrival in the outlying districts took longer, it was on the scene and on most people's minds. The new County Intermediate School in Bridgend heralded a bright new beginning with evening continuation schools,[12] as they were called, providing cookery and other useful lessons for mature students at the end of school days. And Betharan Chapel, as ever, was a source of inspiration to the Howell family, where its new vestry, the place of Sarah Jane's Sunday school, was now being put to another use.

---

[12]   *The Glamorgan Gazette,* periodic School Reports: Bridgend Library Services.

Cricket had arrived in the village, and this is where the club's committee usually met.[13] Sometimes, it was to arrange refreshments and social functions for the team, but usually it was to arrange matches. Cricket was seizing the villagers' attention whilst bringing competitive sport, formality, and a sense of gentlemanly fellowship to the local sports field. Besides the usual inter-village rivalry, a respected councillor or other leading dignitary occasionally raised a team to challenge the 'chosen eleven' of another well-known figure in the district such as the local doctor. This was good fun for all, although it was meant to be kept within its boundaries, as the following snippet from *The Glamorgan Gazette,* of September 16th 1898 suggests:

> It is very painful to observe a group of young men spending their Sunday afternoon sitting about on the common conversing on matters respecting the cricket matches played on the previous day, instead of attending Sunday school. Young men, take my advice and reform!

This article would have amused the household at Abergarw where, from the farmhouse windows, Sarah Jane and her sisters enjoyed watching Uncle Jenkin herding the cattle round the front of the yard at the end of the day. They also accompanied him when feeding the animals, taking it in turns to hold the lantern during dark winter nights, something that Beatrice often referred to in later life.

---

[13]   *The Glamorgan Gazette,* April 29th 1898: Bridgend Library Services.

Meanwhile, Sarah Jane and Katie could not wait to get home from Bryncethin School, where they sometimes found their mother plucking chickens ready for the Saturday market. By now, Beatrice had become protective towards young Margot, although she dropped her guard one day, when a gander caught hold of her little sister by the coat, as if to drag her away.

Incidents of this nature rolled the weeks and months forward towards the next century when better travel and communications would bring people closer together from distant lands. However, contrary to expectations, the country was entering into the grip of the Boer War, which saw men from the district enrolling at the local Drill Hall in Bridgend and enduring weeks of sailing before standing amidst warfare on the open veldts of South Africa. And with them were hundreds of horses that might otherwise have been traded on the mountain-top location of St Mary Hill Fair overlooking Bridgend.

Although these troubles were far away, *The Glamorgan Gazette* brought the day's action home with 'Letters from the Front' sent by serving soldiers to loved-ones back in Bridgend. Bullets, bayonets, and modern rifles made for bloody encounters in the deep trenches, with serious loss of lives. A lack of water, and the dreaded enteric sickness, made conditions even more difficult as horse-drawn ambulance carts worked around the clock taking soldiers away for treatment. One of the news bulletins described the ordeals facing the men, even during the days between combat:

> After the first fight, we started at once on the march,
> day and night, mostly without anything to eat half our
> time. Every now and then a few of the weaker ones
> would drop out ... [14]

Another letter found its way up the steep river valley to
nearby Blaengarw from the vicinity of Kimberley, just a few
days march from a heavily-mined diamond reserve. The
author wrote of the oppressive daytime heat and the cold of
night before the men faced the Boers in prolonged battles,
sometimes lasting up to fourteen hours. Here are more
chilling thoughts from this young man who had been
brought up only miles away from Brynmenyn and whose
life was under threat:

> War is an awful thing; no one would credit it, only
> those who are in the midst of it. If my life is spared,
> I shall be able to explain to you better when I see you.
> Our lives at present are in great danger, the same as
> working underground; but life at all times is not sure.
>
> The Lord hath kept me so far and, if it is *His* will,
> he will bring me through the remainder. I daresay we
> may have several battles before you get this letter but, if
> you notice the papers, you will see whether I am killed
> or wounded. [15]

At home in Abergarw and throughout the community,
these words were felt with sadness, whilst in Betharan
Chapel prayers went out to all concerned – as volunteers
exercised on the homeland awaiting their own call to duty.

---

[14]   *The Glamorgan Gazette*, April 27th 1900: Bridgend Library Services.
[15]   *The Glamorgan Gazette*, January 26th 1900: Bridgend Library Services.

As war savings contributed to soldier comforts, and parcels were despatched to the battle scenes, everyone hoped for an end to the fighting so that there would be a speedy return home for the men. Meanwhile, miles away, the chimes of Big Ben would soon be ringing amidst scenes of street chaos and coronation-like celebrations. And, as a century disappeared in the excitement, washed down with potent local brews, it was time for a new tomorrow. It would bring unparalleled innovation and a wealth of wonderment – but, amidst hope and great expectations, there would be more tears of sadness along the way.

A Taste of Bristol and the
Joys of Clifton Down

BRISTOL IN THE EARLY 1900S was a thriving, cultured, and well-to-do city. Of course, it had developed as a sea port for hundreds of years, during which time profitable maritime trading had laid the foundations for later prosperity and affluence. Each of the tall sailing ships that survived the choppy waters of the Bristol Channel brought with them much needed cargoes from far away parts, often tea, sugar and tobacco, whilst exports of wool, grain, and other produce were sent back in return. Now, Bristol had become a commanding city: offering trade, employment, shipping, shops, and rail links. It also had a vibrant hinterland and architecture to boast about.

For George Howell, Bristol offered something else, for in recent years it had become recognised as a centre of learning. This was largely due to John Percival, headmaster of Clifton College, an esteemed independent school for boys[16] who, as a brilliant academic, had between 1862 and 1878 raised the profile of teaching in Bristol at a time when smaller private boarding schools were being put in place for girls. Sarah Jane's father knew that besides offering a good choice of lessons, these schools attached importance to the

---

[16]   *Who Was Who* Volume II 1916 – 1928, A & C Black, London:
       Carmarthenshire Library Services.

development of their pupils' character. They were effectively 'finishing schools;' they took pains to instil confidence, to challenge ambition and to nurture potential.

Amongst the family members at Abergarw, Bristol was known for different reasons. Evan was aware of the docks during the earlier slave trade. Those were sad days but times had moved on, and the old warehouses were still standing and, no doubt, were equally packed to the rafters with seafaring goods. Evan had been a boy when the *SS Great Britain* was built in Bristol, another example of Mr Brunel's genius, a finely propelled steamer, fired by coal, daring, dashing and ready to ride the waves. For Evan's son, Jenkin, Bristol meant the rich green dairy pastureland adjoining a vibrant city and the hullabaloo of market days when everyone directed their animals towards the marts. Not surprisingly, Jenkin had also heard a thing or two about the local inns, as well as the malt and hops that flavoured the West Country ale.

From early times, travelling from Cardiff to Bristol used to involve the splash and romance of a channel crossing, before steam locomotives wound their way around Gloucestershire on a cross-country route. But the arrival of the Severn Railway passage made the journey easier for Sarah Jane, and the light that emerged at the end of the tunnel shone towards a sea of English greenery, broken by houses and hamlets of thick thatch-roof appeal. What a joy rail travel had become: locomotives winding their way through forests and woodlands, over rivers and roads and, on a hot summer's day, into fields at harvest time, close enough to smell and almost touch the hay. Women and girls would be raking the golden strands into little hay cocks, as men and boys with hand pikes and pitch-forks hoisted the tumps onto the load. This was farming at its best and all so reminiscent of days in Abergarw when, amidst great happiness, picnic baskets were brought into the field and the feasting began.

Temple Meads was already a railway station of great appeal, its architecture giving rise to a clock tower and the feel of importance as passengers and pedestrians milled around the concourse with a spring in their steps. This is where drivers and firemen clambered from footplates as boy-porters and platform attendants carried cases and piled their trolleys high. Outside in the cobbled enclosure, carters pulled up alongside the entrance, jostling for a position near the walkway – but it was in the main thoroughfare that Sarah Jane boarded a local train to Clifton Down only a few miles away.

There are many jewels in Bristol's crown, but Clifton is one of its most precious. Positioned on the lofty grounds overlooking Avon gorge, it brings to this location a mixture of town and countryside besides a touch of class. In one of its corners stands Christ Church, its tower tall, erect and rocket-shaped, as if ready to be launched, whilst in another, the wonders of Clifton Suspension Bridge are draped daringly across the skyline. Clifton provides the perfect picture: multi-shaded stonework; town houses; tree-lined streets; feature fountains, and miles of grassland known as Clifton Down.

Top left:
George and Jennet Howell,
Sarah Jane's parents.
*Photo: a postcard image produced by
Ernest Carver, Bridgend.*

Top right:
Evan Morgan, Sarah Jane's
grandfather, with his
customary white ruff.

Bottom right:
Bosom pals - with sister,
Katie, who is standing.
*Photo: Edwin Lott, Nolton Studio,
Bridgend, another postcard
presentation.*

Photos: courtesy of Janet Moody

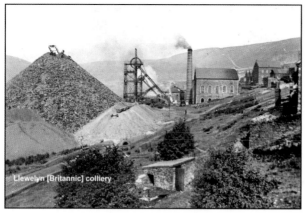

Concentrated mining in the Bridgend district as known to the Howell family.

Photo: courtesy of Wyndham Jones of Gilfach Goch

... and today's
Bedford Park,
Cefn Cribwr,
a reminder of
Glamorgan's
proud industrial
past.

The humpback bridge that Jenkin crossed to get to the Miller's Arms,
with Abergarw farmstead, and house, appearing in the background.

Photo: from the Francis Frith Series, Janet Moody's collection

Top: The Fox and Hounds Hotel, Brynmenyn, alongside the railway crossing. Betharan Chapel can be seen in the background.
Photo: courtesy of Bridgend Library Services

Middle: The Sentinel delivery lorries of Abergarw Brewery, which replaced the horse-drawn carts, complete with solid wheels and open cabins.
Photo: courtesy of Bridgend Library Services

Bottom: ... and the bottle of beer that George Howell forgot to drink!
Photo: courtesy of Janet Moody

The setting of St Mary Hill Fair, a major social event during Sarah Jane's lifetime and, for those who missed the day, 'a calamity in their brief existence,' according to *The Glamorgan Gazette* of April 29th 1890.

Nearby is St Mary's Church, situated alongside the former Bell Inn, a convenient resting place for those who drunk themselves to sleep!

Clifton High School for Girls, a highly respected establishment situated near to the location of Sarah Jane's boarding school. In this picture the girls are playing cricket whilst, inset, a small party of scholars are seen enjoying a day's outing.

Photos: courtesy of Clifton High School

Bridgend, a pretty market town when Sarah Jane, a teenager, began duties as a Pupil Teacher. Pictured in the middle-right is the corner of Caroline Street and, above, the Market Hall, whilst here is an even earlier image of Bridgend Railway station circa 1850.

Photos: courtesy of Bridgend Library Services

Tynyrheol Primary School, Llangeinor, where Sarah Jane worked between August 1906 and April 1910 .

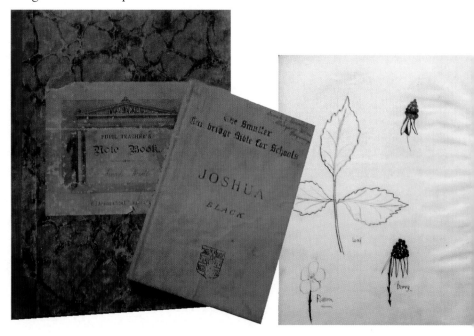

Sarah Jane's Pupil Teacher's exercise book and the book of *Joshua* to which she often referred, inscribed with her name and address. The drawing above and the writing on the following page are examples of Sarah Jane's work.

Thanks to Janet Moody

St Theodore's Church, Bryncethin, Sarah Jane's
favourite place of worship © *The Francis Frith Collection*
and here she is looking elegant and beautiful in her
Sunday-best.   *Photo: Janet Moody*

Sarah Jane passed through Blackmill
Railway Station on her way to Gilfach Goch
thanks to Leslie Allen and Ogmore Valley Historical Society
... and there was no shortage of admirers
when she stepped off the train!
another classic from Wyndham Jones' collection

To get to school in Gilfach Goch, Sarah Jane walked along a footpath from the railway station to Evanstown, seeing Saint Barnabas Church (on the left) in the distance.

Photos:
courtesy of Wyndham Jones

Two typical views of the mining community which the school served so well.

Abercerdin School which enjoys a spectacular view of the wide and open valley.

Abergarw House, once a showpiece property in Brynmenyn, situated alongside the old road to Llangeinor and during Sarah Jane's later days when hardly a car was seen.

Photos: Janet Moody's collection

Isabella   Ronald

Bertie

Dorothy

Ynysawdre Parish Hall, which remains unaltered throughout all the years, where Sarah Jane reported to work on that fateful morning, Tuesday December 19th 1911.

above:
Young Bertie Gubbins appears on the left of this photograph with his brother and two sisters.

The collection of Peter Evans, Bertie's nephew.

left:
A view of the Llynfi River from the bridge near Ynysawdre Parish Hall. Sarah Jane travelled this course as she struggled for her life, before being found more than a quarter of a mile downstream on an island of small pebbles.

In Loving Memory

OF

SARAH JANE HOWELL,

ELDEST DAUGHTER OF GEORGE AND JENNET
HOWELL, ABERGARW FARM, BRYNMENYN,

Assistant Mistress at Brynmenyn
Council School,

*Who lost her life in the Llynfi
River, in saving one of the Pupils
from drowning on the
19th of December, 1911.*

———o———

Interred at the Burial Ground of the Betharran
Congregational Chapel, Brynmenyn,
22nd of December, 1911.

———o———

"Greater love hath no man than this, that a
man lay down his life for his friends."

JOHN XV., 13.

The official Bereavement Notice which has been adapted to form the front and
back cover of this book.

SOUTH WALES DAILY NEWS. SATURDAY. DECEMBER 23. 1911.

BURIAL OF A WELSH HEROINE: FUNERAL SCENES AT BRYNMENYN.

The South Wales Daily News dated Saturday December 23rd 1911 shows pictures
of the funeral cortege, Abergarw farmhouse and the children who mourned
their teacher, Sarah Jane.

Here are the sad scenes, courtesy of Janet Moody's newspaper cutting.

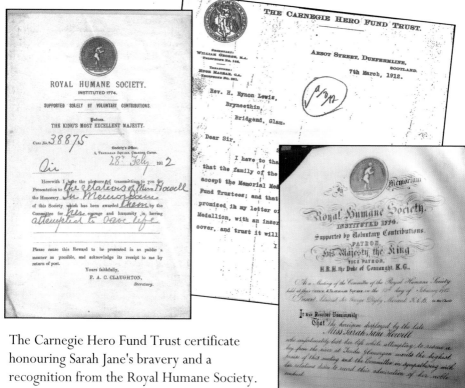

The Carnegie Hero Fund Trust certificate honouring Sarah Jane's bravery and a recognition from the Royal Humane Society.
Janet Moody

Brynmenyn School which was opened on January 13th 1913 and where Sarah Jane was meant to teach.
The Francis Frith Collection and provided by Janet Moody

Today's Bryngarw Hotel and Country Park situated only a short walk away: the perfect place for nature studies and once the home of Captain Onslow Powell Traherne.

The day George and Jennet treated the teachers and staff of Brynmenyn School to afternoon tea. All five of Sarah Jane's sisters appear in the photograph.

above left: the Howell family and friends gather at the school premises on January 16th 1915, the day the Sarah Jane Memorial was unveiled.

above right: A school caretaker attends to the bronze memorial, long before the small statue was torn from its plinth in the summer of 1970.

inset... and the beautiful detail of the floral plaque that was a part of the presentation.   *All photos are from Janet Moody's collection*

During her lifetime, Margot, the fourth born of the Howell daughters and a teacher at Brynmenyn, was often invited back to the school to present the Sarah Jane Howell annual award. Here she is in the late 1970s - and what an impressive scene! *Brynmenyn Primary School's collection*

A distant view of Abergarw House and the nearby terrace of three houses built by Sarah Jane's father, George Howell. His other two building projects, today's, Glanyrafon and Glendale, are located near to where the photograph was taken.

St Cein's Church and Jenkin's grave, together with a view of the open hills from Jenkin's place of rest.

Photos: Janet Moody

The Fox and Hounds today with a glimpse of the disused railway crossing gates. This former hotel was the hub of village life in Brynmenyn for well over a century and it is still a popular public house.

We can imagine the kind face in the front row, (extreme left) belonging to 'Young Bertie' - for here is Bertram Gubbins senior, his father, pictured alongside his wife at a family wedding.

Photo: Peter Evans, Bertie's nephew

Right: The Medical Fund Hospital, Swindon, where 'our' Bertie was admitted before he died in March 1948.

Swindon Central Library, with thanks to Dawn Osborne and with the kind permission of Tim Midwinter

Sarah Jane's family: parents, George and Jennet are seated with Katie and Mattie, in front of Margot, Marjorie and Beatrice.

Photos: Janet Moody

Unfortunately, no photographs can be shown of the wonderful scene in Brynmenyn Primary School's Central Hall when pupils, teachers, governors and friends gathered for the Memorial Assembly commemorating the centenary of Sarah Jane's drowning.

However, here is the Order of Service, the author's personal invitation and, a 'family favourite' of our 'Welsh Heroine' as we will always remember her.

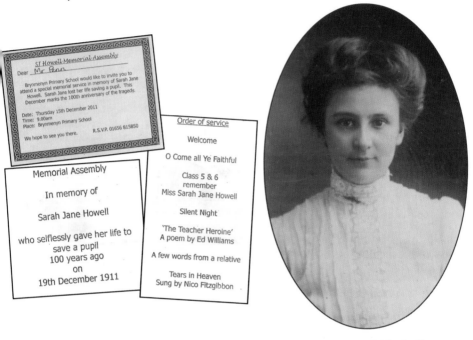

SJ Howell Memorial Assembly

Dear Mr Penn

Brynmenyn Primary School would like to invite you to attend a special memorial service in memory of Sarah Jane Howell. Sarah Jane lost her life saving a pupil. This December marks the 100th anniversary of the tragedy.

Date: Thursday 15th December 2011
Time: 9.00am
Place: Brynmenyn Primary School

We hope to see you there.   R.S.V.P. 01656 815850

Memorial Assembly

In memory of

Sarah Jane Howell

who selflessly gave her life to save a pupil
100 years ago
on
19th December 1911

Order of service

Welcome

O Come all Ye Faithful

Class 5 & 6
remember
Miss Sarah Jane Howell

Silent Night

'The Teacher Heroine'
A poem by Ed Williams

A few words from a relative

Tears in Heaven
Sung by Nico Fitzgibbon

Betharan, a much photographed building since its beginning in 1809. Sadly, however, it is no longer a chapel, although Sarah Jane's tall headstone can still be seen near the main entrance.

Sarah Jane was one of many young girls privileged to receive education at this setting. Boarding schools adorned the township, being often large residences, where accommodation and facilities were shared. In many cases they were owned by the lady-teacher who sometimes lived alone or, perhaps, with a servant or helper. Whiteladies Road was a popular centre for these schools, and so also were many of the green-shaded side-streets that led into it. They offered a cosy atmosphere for learning, where fireside bookwork and lessons could be enjoyed, and it is in this sheltered existence, free from distractions, that Sarah Jane found peace-and-quiet away from home. And like many young ladies of tomorrow – the daughters of ambitious parents and well-to-do physicians, lawyers, businessmen, artisans and the like – she settled into her new routines.

Whilst these independent schools varied slightly in terms of objectives and priorities, they all tended to offer a wholesome preparation for the next stage of life. English and recitation benefited Sarah Jane, a Welsh-speaker, and there would be time aplenty for this. Letter writing was also encouraged: a skilful art conveying attitudes and feelings between the lines accompanied by the hope of a suitable reply following in the post. An appreciation of music had its rightful place in a meaningful itinerary, whilst manners, morals, ethics and prayers mattered, and all found their way onto the white tablecloths at meal times.

It was during these early years of the new century that a lady by the name of Miss Emma Hobbs was running a 'High

Class School for Girls in Clifton.[17] Having earlier taught in the Cothamside district, she had by the year 1900 moved to one of the elegant stone-faced residences known as Charente, Chantry Road, in the centre of Clifton.[18] By coincidence, another lady, Mrs Jane Hobbs, who may have been a relative, was running the Marlborough House Girl's School a walk away at 23 Whiteladies Road.[19] It is believed that Sarah Jane was known to both these ladies[20] whilst, in all probability, she attended the first mentioned school where, during autumn's golden tinge, the curtains were pulled back to reveal falling leaves whirling around the front enclosure in the wind. Both catered for only a few boarders, and were advertised in the *Bristol and Suburban Trades Directory*. In particular, Marlborough House Girls School, aimed ...

> to impart a sound and liberal education to the pupils, whilst combining careful training and school discipline with home comforts and advantages.[21]

To vary routines, ladies of the district were accustomed to visit the house to address the girls. Conversations and debates would arise and everyone was encouraged to join in. Likewise, there would be outings, usually to the residences of the teacher's friends. These might involve a walk to the parish of Redland, or a ride in the open cart,

---

[17] *Bristol and Suburban Names Directory*, 1902.
  Bristol Central Library Services and the British Census 1901.
  Web Site www Find MyPast: June 30th 2014.
[18] Please see (17) above – and a visit to Chantry Road, Clifton by the author.
[19] Please see reference (17) above.
[20] *The Glamorgan Gazette* of December 29th 1911: Bridgend Library Services.
[21] Web site www. Bristol Information: June 30th 2014.

whilst occasionally the girls would jump aboard a train for a taste of city life. Besides offering new experiences, these mini excursions developed team spirit, sharing and social skills which, alongside volumes of bookwork and some games, provided a rounded education.

One of Clifton's better-known boarding schools is today's Clifton High School, which was founded in 1877 for girls. Situated just a walk away from Whiteladies Road, and accommodating ambitious pupils, the reception area of this beautiful property still features bright mosaic flooring. In the days of Sarah Jane, this entrance would have looked out onto the front lawn, where the girls, wearing full length white dresses and flat straw hats, assembled to watch colleagues playing their own version of cricket and other games in the summer months.

At this same school the annual awards ceremony took on a special meaning from early days when a distinguished guest distributed certificates. In 1902, the Right Honourable H.H. Asquith, K.C. M.P. visited the school. No doubt, this was Herbert Henry Asquith, who as Prime Minister presided over Britain's entry into the Great War. But, a few years earlier, it was the turn of Professor Lloyd Morgan, Principal of University College, Bristol.[22] This gentleman gave an outstanding address, one that challenged the girls to aim high for success in life.

Encouraging members of his audience to broaden their intelligence, Professor Lloyd Morgan recommended that

---

[22] An Address delivered to school pupils on October 27th 1896: Clifton High School Archives.

more questions be asked in their daily lives. He challenged everyone to study a range of subjects; to delve searchingly into topics; to find reason to emulate heroes, and to know more about famous people, especially literary scholars such as Shakespeare, Chaucer, Milton and Tennyson. He emphasised that the girls represented the school and that they each had a responsibility to serve others. Above all, he stressed the need to acquire knowledge through 'taking an interest,' a subject that was Professor Lloyd Morgan's first lesson that day:

> Without *interest* you will never make much progress in anything... but if you will be constantly on the look-out for the points of *interest* and dwell upon them, it is surprising how the *interest* will spread and diffuse itself over the whole subject.

Next, he challenged each student to influence their destinies through being constructive: 'It is this constructiveness which I want you to foster and develop and train to good purposes,' he said, adding that the knowledge gained from school subjects will amount to building blocks for later life. And they are for 'building houses, and art galleries and, I venture to add, churches,' he stated before illustrating this same point:

> Given a thousand bricks, you may, either, make a heap of them and sit uncomfortably on the top of it, or you may build them into a house or cottage according to your intellectual means and live comfortably inside it. I should advise you to build a tenement, and not sit outside in the cold.

These were stirring words as Professor Lloyd Morgan carried his message in a different direction. 'Historical facts,' he stated, should be explored by scholars so that they can be slotted into a fuller and complete 'picture.' 'But remember this,' he added, 'you have to paint your own historical picture. Or, more generally, you have to build your own intellectual and moral edifice.' Then, when providing a brief résumé, he concluded his lesson on the art of learning and of life by suggesting that members of his audience enhance their powers of imagination to ensure that learning is 'fused into harmony and raised to its highest level.'

As Sarah Jane tried her hardest in work and play to respond to similar ideals, Sundays came round quickly. And, as in Brynmenyn, this is when she and her colleagues attended a local church where she sat amongst friends and strangers in fellowship and prayers. Then, that special moment of the week arrived when, regardless of the weather, it was customary to dress for a ramble across the 'Down.' Exhilarated by the fresh sea air blowing up the estuary from the mouth of the channel, these occasions perambulating across the famous green expanse reminded Sarah Jane of the passing of time. Each jaunt triggered an awareness that end-of-term holidays were drawing nearer, when she would jump aboard the next train out of Bristol, heading home, again, to Wales.

Home Sweet Home and on to
the Teaching Trail

SARAH JANE'S EXPERIENCES IN CLIFTON provided the perfect stepping stone for a quantum-leap in life. This favourite village had been a treasure trove but the memories and friendships would continue. Many people had influenced Abergarw's young scholar in shaping her thoughts and attitude whilst giving her the confidence and skills to move on. Mrs Bradley, a lady of high standing who lived in the village of Bitton, outside Bristol, was one of these,[23] and the qualities she recognised would one day be revealed to all.

Sarah Jane was returning home when women were conquering the world. Queen Victoria's passing a few years earlier highlighted her enterprise and efficiency during an amazing run of success. Florence Nightingale was another: a leader and visionary, strong enough to challenge the authorities and to make her mark. She had opened the door to nursing, and now the country beckoned candidates to walk in. Sarah Jane's homeland was already rising to the challenge as young ladies, having been trained by strict matrons, joined the Bridgend Nursing Association. Moving from one patient to the next on a bicycle or by pony and

---

[23] *The Glamorgan Gazette*, February 9th 1912: Bridgend Library Services.

trap, they provided welcome support for overworked doctors struggling to cope with their considerable demands. But Sarah Jane's preference was to teach, and little stopped her once she had made up her mind. Reaching for her lesson books and ink pen, preparations began in earnest, whilst qualifications were to follow further down the line.

By now Sarah Jane was the eldest of six daughters: Mattie, having been born in 1901, with Marjorie, who followed two years later, now a baby in her cot. Mother, Jennet, had her work cut out but was the portly picture of happiness in her full-fronted cooking apron, removing pastries from the oven, and sampling them, of course. Jennet had plenty of helpers, and Katie, Beatrice and Margot all pitched into their allotted tasks after school. George's terraced houses caught everybody's eye as he considered his next project, which was to replace the dilapidated labourer's cottage adjacent to this modern row and opposite the farm entrance, with another brand new dwelling. Evan's presence was sadly missed; his fireside chair would never be the same and the old tales had gone – whilst Jenkin, having assumed his father's voting rights and ultimately his authority, could be forgiven for assuming just a hint of importance as he widened his gait.

It is hardly surprising that it was another culture shock for Sarah Jane when returning home. Whiteladies Road in Clifton and Abergarw Road in Brynmenyn are worlds apart. It would take more than modern engineering to bridge this gap, and it was inevitable that comparisons would be made. But, in returning, Sarah Jane could enjoy all that Bridgend offered.

Sitting in gently-rolling countryside, connected to rivers and waterways, it had developed into a beautiful little town, enhanced by the individual identities of its many constituent parishes. Besides livestock sales and market hall provisions, open air trade stands appeared on the central 'Green,' in amongst a variety of small family-run shops. Only a walk away is the wide expanse of Newbridge Fields — surely Bridgend's answer to Clifton Down — where parents and children still while away happy hours relaxing or participating in a bracing walk. Across the meadows beyond the river bridges, Merthyr Mawr exudes the post-card image of a quaint thatched-roof hamlet whilst, all around, Bridgend's open fields and countryside frame its bigger picture.

Penybont ar Ogwr (meaning Bridgend on the river Ogmore) had, of course, its own fifteenth-century river bridge, much celebrated too, 'Yr Hen Bont,' (The Old Bridge) complete with kicking stones to prevent cart and carriage wheels from colliding with its walls. The bridge was once a multi-arched work of art, designed to link two earlier settlements. One was **New**castle, where the castle ruins remain today and, the other, **Old**castle, situated in the Nolton area of town. Once, an essential gateway into Bridgend from Laleston and the west, the bridge is still a fine feature in the town today despite having lost one or two of its original arches during heavy floods.[24]

It is from this ancient structure that Sarah Jane and her family once walked, looking down onto a riverbank

---

[24]   Web site: www. The Bridgend Bridge, June 30th 2014.

of silted stones where ducks dunked their heads as they swam around, and casual observers sat on the water's edge when the weather was fine. Around the corner, the town, fully self-sufficient in the way of general goods, basic needs and a lot more, was a busy place with lime kilns, foundries, quarries, agricultural stores, tanneries and a brewery. The Wyndham, a proud and imposing hotel, was a popular meeting place whilst outside its crowded bars horse and carts, masters and errand boys, shoppers, traders, travelling merchants and visitors from nearby valleys and villages filled the streets. All wound their way through the cobbled enclosures, side-stepping boys who scraped horse droppings into little barrows and passing friendly police officers in smart helmets and full length coats, but with a serious truncheon tucked inside.

Bridgend's central location and connections to the Great Western Railway terminals and valley lines, made it convenient to visit places such as Merthyr Tydfil where during 1905, the year of Sarah Jane's return to Brynmenyn, the National Eisteddfod was staged in nearby Aberpennar (Mountain Ash). This would have interested Abergarw's budding teacher, not only for the poetry, singing and drama competitions in the Welsh language and the *Gorsedd* crowning of the bards – but because its venue was near to the birth place of her grandfather, John Howells.[25] Besides being a blacksmith, he was a respected mathematician who

---

[25] The family name, as earlier mentioned, was reduced to 'Howell.'

taught at night school in Abercanaid[26] and he was proud to conduct the Merthyr United Choir at a time when choristers in their droves emerged from the bowels of the earth to rejoice in the fellowship of music and song as they reached the top notes.

For Mr Howells' granddaughter, these were now exciting days in the rather different teaching world of council schools and Sarah Jane had earned her chance. Reverend Eynon Lewis, Pastor of Betharan, was a close friend of the Howell family and he knew of their long association with the chapel. He had shared some pleasant times with George and Jennet and the girls, and remembered Sarah Jane attending the Band of Hope activities as a child. Reverend Eynon Lewis, an upstanding gentleman of the cloth, was also one of the managers at Bryncethin Infants School, a role that carried responsibility for teaching appointments.[27] Sarah Jane was in good company and if she had needed a helping hand she was well placed for a little divine intervention at this minister's behest. Of course, all the while Reverend Eynon Lewis and his colleagues monitored the children's response to the teachings and underlying disciplines of Scripture, such was its continued importance, as well as hymn singing.

At this time, pupil teachers were given the opportunity of learning directly from school headmasters or

---

[26] *The Glamorgan Gazette*, February 23rd 1912:
      Bridgend Library Services.
[27] Bryncethin National Infants School Log Book (1884 – 1907):
      Glamorgan Archive Services.

headmistresses. In many respects, this was the perfect situation because the 'Head's' experience was passed on at first hand, whilst pupil teachers were released periodically to the local 'Central Classes,' such as those held at Tondu, for training.[28] Later there would be examinations to sit so as to qualify as assistant mistresses or masters. In some instances, pupil teachers had a rather abrupt awakening to their duties during staff shortages when, having already demonstrated leadership and academic abilities, they were invited to step in front of the class.[29] Then, trusting they had the determination to progress, they were given help by the head teacher to develop their potential.

These days were, of course, severely demanding. Many children and teachers had to walk long distances to school and, in the howling gales of a dark winter's morning they arrived soaked to the skin. The school stove was the only heating available and if it failed to function, or lacked fuel, it was usual for everyone to be sent home. Of course, epidemics arrived in serious proportions and claimed lives, and with classes generally overfull, the head teachers had a lot of manoeuvring to do when striving to meet expected demands.

Little was overlooked, however, and the Log Book records were dutifully completed. In March 1905, the inspector's report for Bryncethin Infants School emphasised

---

[28] Bryncethin National Infants School Log Book (1884 – 1907): Glamorgan Archive Services.

[29] Bryncethin National Infants School Log Book (1884 – 1907): Glamorgan Archive Services.

the need to improve the staffing. This promptly precipitated a movement of teachers between neighbouring schools, paving the way for a new mistress. Two months later, Sarah Jane had arrived on the scene, aged just fifteen, to work under the direction of Mr Higgins, the headmaster. From this time, Sarah Jane featured in the Log Book,[30] and here are a few entries describing the school's activities immediately before and after she arrived:

June 13th 1904
The attendance this morning is wretchedly bad; one cause, I am told, is the miners' demonstration at Porthcawl.

February 23rd 1905
Mr Higgins has ordered 5 cwt. of coal. The weather is bitterly cold, and on Monday there were no fires at all in school.

January 11th 1906
Sarah J. Howell is away for three days at the Centre – so I am without assistance for three days of the whole week.

March 30th 1906
Sarah J. Howell has been acknowledged by the Council since March 20th at a salary of £5 per annum.

March 9th 1906 (Minister's Report)
I visited the school this afternoon. The weather being fine – there were 67 present out of a possible 72. All seemed to be in good order. [Reverend] H. Eynon Lewis.

---

[30] Bryncethin National Infants School Log Book (1884 – 1907): Glamorgan Archive Services.

Beginning her teaching career in Bryncethin in the warmth of late Spring meant that Sarah Jane enjoyed seeing the hedgerows bursting into life and colour with fresh green stems and stalks. During the course of a mile and a half walk from Abergarw farm, she gathered invaluable teaching material, which she later wrote in neat long-hand in her Pupil Teacher's Note Book. This classic workbook – produced by E.J. Arnold & Son Ltd, recognised educational publishers – was hard-covered, well-bound and priced at 'one shilling' and came with alternate plain and lined pages. It was intended for 'oral, object and general lesson notes' and, inside, Sarah Jane described her subject before providing illustrative drawings on the opposite page. Many passages related to nature studies, and one referred to oak apples. Here are some of Sarah Jane's words on the subject:

> A tiny insect settles on a small twig of the oak [and] makes a tiny hole in it. There she lays her eggs, covering them over with juice which she squeezes from her body. Oak apples grow round eggs, each being in a tiny chamber by itself. After some time, eggs are hatched. The [emerging] grubs feed on the oak apples [and] develop into flies [usually gall flies or wasps]. Oak apples are reddish brown in colour and round in shape.

When Sundays came round at the end of busy weeks, Sarah Jane made a similar walk to Bryncethin to attend St Theodore's Church. As a regular member of the congregation and a Sunday school teacher she was, effectively, breaking family tradition by choosing to hear sermons in English as opposed to Betharan's Welsh.

At St Theodore's, Sarah Jane gave her regular tithe and this was a generous offering considering that her earnings as an unqualified teacher were small, and only a portion of what male colleagues received for doing similar work with comparable responsibilities.

As a rule, chapel sermons were then strongly delivered messages which drew great commitment and dedication from regular members determined to uphold their faith. Right was right, wrong was wrong; there was little middle ground. Pregnancy, for instance, falling outside of wedlock was viewed as a serious sin and brought severe repercussions. The shame and embarrassment of the woman's family and church were usually too much to bear, necessitating a swift relocation of the perceived offender to Bristol or further afield to be out of the way. With religion filtering into the local newspapers, *The Glamorgan Gazette* of September 16th 1898 published an interesting message whereby the preacher linked the 'sowing of a seed' and the 'reaping of a fruit,' to the greater spiritual world. Below is a small extract of his message, which includes the words of Sir John Lubbock, Liberal politician, that were thought provoking at the time and are still relevant to this day:

> We cannot break the laws of a wise and benevolent God without paying the penalty... We take a punishment for our sins. Who punishes us? We punish ourselves. The world is so arranged that goodness brings joy, and evil sorrow. To sin, and not to suffer, would involve an interference with the laws of nature.

Sarah Jane's commitment to Bible studies had steadily continued over the years whilst sitting happily in a quiet corner of the farmhouse or on one of her father's home-made wooden benches under the trees, allowing the written word to enter into her deepest thoughts. One of her much-treasured books tells the story of *Joshua*, part of a series entitled *The Smaller Cambridge Bible for Schools*. It is a pocket-sized book with impressive reviews, each beautifully written inside and, without doubt, these had at one time caught Sarah Jane's eye. The *Sunday School Chronicle* stated that 'no better commentaries' could be presented to scholars and candidates sitting scripture examinations, whilst an Educational Review could not recommend 'better little manuals' for use in schools and for private reading.

Throughout the text, Sarah Jane made light markings in pencil, sometimes underlining words or sentences as well as conveying her thoughts with some revealing notes that emphasised her grasp of the subject. These are the rather telling words she wrote about the book's title which she suggests is attributable to *Joshua* for the reasons that...

It commences with the period at which Joshua begins to lead the people.

It deals with the history of the people of Israel under Joshua's leadership.

It ends with the death of Joshua.

As regards its author, Sarah Jane made the following comment...

> [There is] some uncertainty about [its] author, but the Jewish writers ascribe it to Joshua, because: Joshua would be likely to keep a record, [just] as Moses did; he alone could give an account of the covenant at Shechem, and he alone could record the personal commands of God.

In Sarah Jane's own personal opinion, however, the work was written by an elder who, she states...

> Out-lived Joshua: since he uses the 1st person [and] because Joshua could not write about his own death, and events which occurred after his death.

In these short statements, Sarah Jane demonstrates great resolve to comprehend the passages, not wanting to continue her reading until the wider meaning of the word had been explored and fully understood. For students of Scripture this, a challenging exercise, may have been a lonely journey, but not for a member of a motivated congregation who shared with friends at St Theodore's happy social times as well as Bible readings. One of the main events in the church's calendar was the Flower Service, when the children carried floral decorations and flags down the streets of Bryncethin whilst a local brass band played trumpets and trombones. This was usually followed by a church service and an afternoon tea when as many as two hundred people attended – whilst the flowers

were put to good use at the cottage hospital and care homes
of Bridgend.

St Theodore's provided the discipline and inspiration
Sarah Jane needed to help her through the classroom weeks.
In April 1906, there were eighty-one scholars registered at
Bryncethin School yet, on occasions, she was the only
teacher present to support her headmaster as he struggled
when, oftentimes, feeling unwell himself. Referring to
further Log Book entries the following month, it was stated
that Mr Higgins was preparing Sarah Jane for examinations.
Days were proving eventful to say the least and, due to
more staff changes, his young pupil teacher was soon
leaving for Llangeinor in the Garw Valley. This is where
Tynyrheol, another recently opened school, was to provide
Sarah Jane's second teaching post.[31]

---

[31]   Bryncethin National Infants School Log Book (1884 – 1907):
       Glamorgan Archive Services.

A Fashionable Young Lady

POOR UNCLE JENKIN had become out-numbered at Abergarw farm by a growing band of young ladies. This was all totally agreeable but these girls were a lively bunch, and one or two of them were dare-devils, too. Beatrice led the way, fearless throughout life, while Mattie, by now a seven year old, was not far behind. They were the type to jump onto a stray pony, riding it bare-back, and without falling-off. Meanwhile, Katie, closer to Sarah Jane in mild manners, temperament and age, was becoming an accomplished musician. Pianoforte lessons up the road at Bryncethin Fawr farm were shaping her for a new career, as members of Betharan recognised that in Katie they had found a long-term organist for the chapel.

During school holidays, Katie liked to spend time staying with her grandmother's family at Cefn Cribwr, a village only a few miles to the south-west of Brynmenyn. This set a precedent for Margot who was noticeably the quietest of the girls so far, despite Marjorie, still only four, capable of changing this. Margot looked forward to her own summer vacation, when she disappeared for spells to Bettws, the next village, where her hostess, Jennet's sister, Catherine, had been renamed *Aunty Bettws* by the girls. It is there on the higher ground, between the Llynfi and Garw rivers, that Margot explored a different stretch of wildlife, taking note of all she found for her own teaching career in later life.

Jennet and George were amused to see the girls dividing themselves into three separate pairings according to their ages and, with there being no shortage of hot tempers amongst them, Sarah Jane was respected for her lady-like qualities. But this did not stop her leading the way when there was farm work to be done, hair tied-back, standing tall, ready to make her presence felt. Of course, farmers' daughters are not usually shy of work and this was true of Jennet's girls who, during the hot summer months, spread themselves around the fields turning the hay with wooden rakes so that it dried in the overhead sun. And, when it was time to carry the crop away, they were alongside Uncle Jenkin as the gambo wobbled back down the hill.

To the world, Sarah Jane looked a typical member of the later Woman's Land Army, all kitted out in dungarees; yet, whenever she changed into her costumes, she was every inch a fashionable young lady. Of course, she knew that ladies were under the spotlight now, for the women's suffrage movement had arrived and was strong, driven by leading members who were fighting for voting rights. But, faced with cabinet ministers who neither listened nor budged, frustrations mounted; and this was to lead to riots and arrests and acts of public disorder.

But as for the girls of Abergarw farm, they preferred to do what women love most, delighting themselves with all that adorned the fashionable shop windows. During school holidays, Sarah Jane wasted no time in jumping aboard one of the Bridgend-bound railway carriages, where *London House* offered a full range of clothes and accessories and was, according to *The Glamorgan Gazette*, 'replete with the latest novelties' and exactly 'what the well-dressed Edwardian lady was wearing in 1907.' No doubt they also supplied a selection of flannelettes, fibres, cashmeres and merino dresses, which were all advertised well, and silk umbrellas as sold up the road by *Cockbill's* for a few shillings or more.

Cowbridge offered another shopping outlet despite there being no easy rail route from Bridgend. As a medieval town of charm, its South Gate, known as Porth Y Felin, dates back hundreds of years and occupies a quiet corner alongside the former Cowbridge Grammar School for Boys. This school had, since 1608, been a forerunner of education in Wales, and today's bell tower and umpteen chimney-stacks share secrets from those earlier times. As for Sarah Jane, the building was synonymous with learning, and its peaceful setting in this quiet corner of Cowbridge was a source of inspiration for anyone making progress in the teaching world.

Sarah Jane wasted little time in becoming established at her new school in Llangeinor, after reporting for duty on Monday, August 27th 1906.[32] The seven minute journey on the old steam train that puffed and panted its way up the steep gradient could not have been more convenient for her, joining the mining workmen heading up the valley.

[32] Tynyrheol Mixed and Infants School Log Book: Glamorgan Archive Services.

Indeed, by the time she had settled in her seat, she would see Tynyrheol School getting closer, situated on a flood-free shelf that backed onto Llangeinor Mountain. This was serious equestrian territory, where huntsmen rode in black hats, smart jackets and jodhpurs, beating the bounds followed by packs of excitable hounds. Well known to Richard Price of Tynton, famous preacher and philosopher, this was also Grandfather Evan's home ground where he used to venture to the two famous landmarks near the top. Occasionally, it was to attend weddings and funerals at St Cein's Church, a place of worship with the feel of 'an old rugged cross on a hill far away' – although its next-door neighbour held greater appeal, beyond the cemetery wall.

This was the Llangeinor Arms: then a typical farmer's inn, where it is said that country folk steered their horses and carts many miles to enjoy its mix of fresh air and fine ale. Evan had sat in front of the big open fire on many a winter's night, whilst the timbers spat noisily, filling the hearth with a roaring glow. Playing two-a-side tip-it or table quoits or discussing the efficiency of thrashing machines, steam engines and Henry Bamford's latest mowers – they all shared the undeniable sense of conquering the world, having reached this distant halt by overcoming one of its steep and winding lanes. Many great stories have been shared about this location, where on a fine day the view stretches to the open sea. The following words from *The Glamorgan Gazette* of January 29th 1897 say so much about the great mystique of this elevated landscape:

> It is Prince of the Hills of Glamorgan, and once
> you get to his breezy crest, all is well with you.

It took Sarah Jane no more than a few minutes to walk to the red brick school where large windows still brighten the classroom mood during dark days and where teachers and pupils glance from the front playground onto a rich green valley towards Bettws across the hills. This strong Welsh speaking establishment, that was not spared scarlet fever soon after Sarah Jane arrived, was geared to a varied time-table that included weaving and clay-modelling. According to the Log Book, the children enjoyed pageants and singing anthems and folk songs, whilst St David's day was celebrated in style with leeks, if not daffodils also. The children were conscientious in work and play, although lessons came to an abrupt end when the local ploughing match took place or when Pontycymmer carnival was held on a hot summer's day.[33]

Sarah Jane arrived at Llangeinor before the onset of autumn, which was a season well-known to her after studying why trees shut down for the winter months. In an extract from another of her written exercises, she explains that by the end of summer, a tree's main function in preparing its seed has been completed, a period when 'fruiting time is over.' Generally, this stage heralds a period of rest throughout the winter when trees effectively enter a sleeping stage. By now, fruits have been dispersed: eaten by

---

[33]   Tynyrheol Mixed and Infants School Log Book entries on February 19th 1908 and July 14th 1909: Glamorgan Archive Services.

birds, gathered-in by people, or blown away by the wind. As the days shorten and darkness spreads, the wind and rain cause leaves to fall, birds to fly away, insects to go in search of warmth and squirrels to make their nests. All of this is covered in her words, and here is a brief extract:

Tree Life in Autumn
A tree is fed with sap from the roots. After working during the summer, the roots want rest. Their work for the tree is done.

Why Leaves Fall
They would hinder the tree – snow storms would increase weight and the branches would break.

How they Fall
Attached to [a] branch by [a] small stalk – [with the] flutter of wind, they are gone. When leaves are on the ground, they act as a quilt for seeds and small plants, e.g. violet and dandelion.

Sarah Jane's notes again indicate understanding and knowledge. In truth, at Tynyrheol School she was lengthening her stride, reaching forward to develop her natural talent, whilst keeping an eye on the next round of written tests during the busy Christmas term:

December 16th 1908
Miss S.J. Howell is away today at Tondu Centre,
preparing for her examination in the next two days.

For the Howell family there was something mildly uplifting about Sarah Jane's placement at Llangeinor. It was as if she was extending Abergarw's boundaries just a little further beyond the top fields – surely Jenkin's dream – and it was not difficult for her father, George, accompanied by Margot and Mattie to meet her from the train. George, often seen around the village on his bicycle – trousers clipped tightly, and short white hair ruffled in the breeze – was now part of the management of the Bryncethin brickworks, where the clay pits of the lower land were turned into essential building materials for the community. As a valuable natural resource, each piece of clay was shaped, baked and hardened, before appearing in full glory in the modern red-brick houses of the day.

Just over the hill at Brynmenyn Common, the village had also been enjoying its own brickworks, where the large crushing houses and kilns produced golden coloured specimens of equal status and as hard as nails, for use in fires, ovens and chimneys. But, having worked for years alongside the local coal mine, there was now speculation about the colliery's closure despite the positive influence of a man named Solomon Andrews. Mr Andrews, a distinguished businessman, who was well respected in the mining industry, was, however, advancing in years and shortly after his death Brynmenyn colliery closed in 1908.[34] This was sad news in the village and resulted in the coal trucks and traction engines grinding to a halt, putting to an end much purposeful activity. During its lifespan, the local miners had conveniently walked to work, but now they were packing up their bags and taking their skills and tools elsewhere.

---

[34] Extract from *The Story of Solomon Andrews and his Family*, by John F. Andrews: Bridgend Library Services.

From Gilfach Goch to Ynysawdre
for the Fleet-footed Sarah Jane

ABERGARW HOUSE was shaping to become a showpiece residence, with pantry, bay-windows and fully furnished bathroom. The builders were looking after George Howell and with the property deemed to be the ideal home there was little wonder why passers-by were stopping to admire this work when travelling through the village of Brynmenyn. But George was not one to rest on his laurels; he was now working to complete a set of two adjoining houses one hundred yards away. These are today's Glan-yr-Afon (bank of the river) and Glendale, both attractive stone-faced homes with trimmings. George's connection with the brickworks was serving him well and, likewise, his family's long-term intentions made good sense.

At the right moment, George and Jennet and the girls planned to cross the road to Abergarw House, which was to be their permanent home. This would allow Jenkin, who was now courting a local lady, more freedom at the farm although his willing band of helpers would hardly be far away. George wanted to gift a house to each of his daughters long before the end of his and Jennet's days. Jennet saw things the same and, having lost her brother, Thomas, to America, she wanted her family near at hand as she and George approached old age.

Brynmenyn was, quite simply, home for George and Jennet and they were both now excited about a new school opening in the village. Scheduled to begin in the Christmas term of 1909, they were pleased that Betharan Chapel was to be its temporary base and that Reverend Eynon Lewis was to be one of its managers.[35] The news was all the more exciting because the Howell family saw a potential teaching post for their eldest daughter. Below is the Log Book entry that marked the school's first day:

> *October 18th 1909*
>
> Brynmenyn Infants School and Standard I opened with an attendance of 45 in the morning, and 48 in the afternoon.[36]

It was cosy in the vestry when the rain lashed down on the chapel roof during wintry days. There was also a sense of fun as the teachers and children made history, putting Brynmenyn on the map. And they could not fail to appreciate the reverence of the chapel, and its capacity for the unexpected as, for instance, when lessons were unavoidably cancelled for a funeral service, or a parish tea. But official schooling had begun and it would continue and progress.

At a time when improved steam ships, motor cars, aeroplanes and long-range radio transmissions were opening up the world, Sarah Jane had a lot to explain to the children

---

[35] Brynmenyn Infants School Log Book (1909 – 1912): Glamorgan Archive Services.

[36] Brynmenyn Infants School Log Book (1909 – 1912): Glamorgan Archive Services.

of her class as she prepared to transfer to another school in the Easter Term of 1910. Abercerdin, situated at Evanstown in Gilfach Goch, a journey of about six miles from the farm, was to provide her next career challenge. This school emanated directly from the coal mining of earlier years and had since grown considerably, with at least two classes catering for sixty children. There was no lack of effort by the young scholars of this hard working location, which was the setting for Richard Llewellyn's celebrated book *How Green was My Valley* (1939). We learn from the school Log Book entries that the children worked diligently at English, Welsh, Geography, Elementary Sciences, and all other main subjects, whilst budding choristers were 'singing sweetly' and in harmony for their music teachers.

Sarah Jane arrived at Abercerdin during a period of staff changes, which saw one of the teachers relocated to Bristol. She found Gilfach Goch to be a somewhat isolated location tucked away amongst the hills with no through-road: in essence, as its name implies, Gifach (a small nook), Goch (red). However, it was, in fact, also a red-hot bed of mining, a raging furnace of activity that rumbled with underground movement and heaved with the heavy foot-fall of labourers, hewers, sawyers, plate-layers, wagoners and other experts of deep excavation work. It is these men who reported for their dangerous daily duties but with a sense of sharing and camaraderie that was unrivalled and understood to miners alone.

At this stage of its existence, the Britannic Merthyr Colliery – which was simply 'The Brit' to the men of this valley – was raising output to higher levels. Now employing some 700 men or more, with numbers due to rise, this was just one of the many local mining works which brought inspectors, police officers, railwaymen, engineers, measurers and hordes of ancillary workers to the area. In terms of proximity to sheer industry, Sarah Jane was virtually stepping onto the production line – and at a most difficult time because mounting tension between colliers and mine owners was soon to explode into ugly scenes and riots, just a couple of miles away in Tonypandy. The demands of sustained output simply consumed this and similar locations, while the horses, railway wagons, tall stacks, mounds of debris, and clouds of smoke provided the hallmarks of a colossal concern. Work had brought men and their families into the village, and the rich seams ensured that they would stay.

Gilfach Goch epitomised a mining community that had developed around the colliery pit and which offered basic needs for daily life. Of course, schooling for the children – as founded around the Dinas Main Colliery and later continued by Llandyfodwg School – had eventually led to the introduction of Sarah Jane's new place of work at Kenry Street in the northern section of the valley's wide expanse.[37]

Sarah Jane was certainly covering some ground and Gilfach Goch was the least accessible of her teaching posts, so far. This meant that she took a train from Brynmenyn station to Blackmill before proceeding along the local line

---

[37] Abercerdin Senior School Log Book (1874 – 1919): Glamorgan Archive Services.

that hugged a tributary of the Ogmore River. At the Hendreforgan halt, the train climbed the gradient for, what appears to be, a rounded mile before stopping at Gilfach Goch's busy station. It was there that Sarah Jane stepped onto the platform, before the train pressed onwards to the higher levels, taking the men to work.

With a sharp walk ahead of her, Sarah Jane ventured onto the pathway that still leads almost directly to the school, leaving behind a cursory glimpse of the bottom end of High Street (then called Gilfach Road)[38] – where the tightly packed terraces and stores climb the gradient as if heading into the distant hills. Next, crossing the little wooden bridge over the Ogwr Fach river, Sarah Jane would have enjoyed the site of Saint Barnabas Church on the nearby hill, a building to look up to in every respect, complete with impressive tower and grand entrance. Bracing herself for the final stretch of her walk, she would see the incline of (the upper stretch of) today's Coronation Road in the approaching distance. Higher still stood Abercerdin School, a commanding figure occupying Evanstown's lofty heights: a true master of all that it surveyed, seemingly propped-up by a green expanse suitable for digging allotments and laying gardens in the spring.

During these warm summer months Sarah Jane enjoyed the challenging morning walk, as well as the return leg when school ended. In the course of her journey home, she studied the wildlife, especially birds as they busied themselves having migrated into the northern hemisphere

---

[38] Maps of Gilfach Goch:
Bridgend Library Services.

for food and warmth to rear their offspring. Being naturally interested in birdlife, Sarah Jane knew this subject in detail and this was evident in a piece of work she prepared describing the 'Migration of Birds.' Explaining that 'most of the birds of passage' feed on insects that take to the warm summer air, she mentioned the chiffchaff, wryneck, nightingale, landrail, swallow, whitethroat, and nightjar, as well as the cuckoo whose arrival comes with a friendly message that we recognise well. Then, referring to the effect of the weather, she stated that:

> Birds, as a rule, prefer to travel with the wind blowing sideways. The prevalence of an unfavourable wind will delay the annual flights, so also will gales [and] stormy weather.
>
> In Norway, if the autumn should be mild and the winter late in setting-in, and berries plentiful – the redwing would prefer staying there, and visit our shores at a later date. [Likewise], if our late summer is interrupted by cold weather which kills off insect life, the swallow leaves our shores earlier than usual.

And, as regards late arrivals, Sarah Jane had this to say:

> The woodcock arrives about the beginning of October, coming to us from the forests of Scandinavia and Russia. The snipes, fieldfares and redwings [arrive] from northern Russia [as well as] many varieties of sea birds, ducks etc. Spring migrants are fairly constant in their arrival, but winter arrivals are not.

When October came round with its early-morning nip, Sarah Jane knew that the less inviting weather was not far away. By chance and good fortune, there was now news of another school opening in Brynmenyn. This was to be Brynmenyn Mixed School, based at the modern Ynysawdre Parish Hall on the way to Tondu where there was a teaching vacancy. Living only a walk away from the premises, this was too good an opportunity to miss – so after seven months at Gilfach Goch, the fleet-footed Sarah Jane, still an un-certificated teacher, was again on the move. With barely enough time to clear her desk and say personal goodbyes, her departure was marked by the following note in the school Log Book:

November 2nd 1910:

'Miss S.J. Howell is transferred from 28th instant to Brynmenyn School.

Sarah Jane's initial duties on home territory saw her settling immediately into her little school at Ynysawdre, even before the ink had dried in the admissions register. The parish 'hall' – although still described on the outside of the building as a 'room' – was literally as we imagine: a small yet surprisingly spacious hall, of red and gold brick design that was built in 1898 following years of planning by councillors, architects, contractors and educational officers. With clever seating arrangements, the hall could accommodate a few classes at the same time with further room to spare. Mr Thomas David Johns was the headmaster and Sarah Jane was one of his team of three assistants – and she, having experienced bigger schools, now saw everything on a more manageable scale which was more comfortable by far. This was Sarah Jane's opportunity to make her mark and she would not squander the chance.

On that momentous first morning, October 31st 1910, a total of sixty-nine children walked through the door, followed by two late arrivals in the afternoon.[39] Soon, ordinary morning drills saw everyone exercising before busy hands scribbled sentences into work books. Reverend Eynon Lewis made his usual inspections, ever obliging and always hoping to report well of all he saw and heard, whilst Nurse Hughes arrived with tips on health and cleanliness to help the children who smiled through their adversity, often with coughs and colds, foot-ache from ill-fitting shoes, and nits from lice-infested hair. Offering hygiene habits to support the day's *Hudson Soaps* was the easy part of her brief which extended to visiting scholars and their parents at home.

When the fine weather arrived in the following year, Sarah Jane led the children on nature rambles down the quiet country lanes. Bryngarw estate was only a short walk away, an ancient mansion with out-buildings, stables and kennels, set amongst acres of countryside with lawns, grassland, trees, woods and running water. It was owned around this time by Captain Onslow Powell Traherne of the Glamorgan Yeomanry, a gentleman who would see from his upstairs windows a never-ending range of colours, surely nature's own fashion parade of the new season's shades. Bluebells stole everyone's attention at this moment, a theme of bright blossom amidst a background of great greenery: a feast for

---

[39]   Brynmenyn Mixed School Log Book (1910 – 1973),
       formerly Ynysawdre Parish Hall School: Glamorgan Archive Services.

innocent young eyes in search of samples for classroom studies.

These 'Object Lessons' as they were called, pleased the children who gathered around their teacher as she stopped along the way. Together, they discussed the main vegetation and the developing ash tree is a subject that Sarah Jane has described and illustrated well in her Note Book. 'Seeds appear in bunches,' she stated, 'known as keys because they hang from a chain. Each key is long and slender [and] consists of a seed enclosed in a case which is prolonged into a wing.' 'It was,' she wrote, 'tawny in autumn' and would soon be taken away by the wind.

No nature study would be complete without a pupil impressing their teacher by scraping around in the soil for an earthworm or two. Sarah Jane also had a lot to say about this little animal, stating that despite having no eyes or teeth, it is sensitive to touch and vibrations, whilst possessing a powerful sense of smell to find food. She knew that its unique structure was essential for survival, allowing it to slither through soil, whilst also ventilating it:

> 'When burrowing, it first stretches its head,' she wrote, 'until it is pointed. Then it forces [itself] down the hole in the soil, [pushing] particles of earth apart. Where the earth is compact, it makes its way by swallowing and gnawing the soil.'

With the teachers and children working well together, Brynmenyn's temporary school at Ynysawdre was proving to be a happy place as everyone welcomed the summer break. But, upon returning for the autumn term, examination work and new challenges lay ahead, which saw a new male teacher arriving on the staff. This was Mr Davies, employed for a higher salary than Sarah Jane's £5 per annum in 1906. This again confirmed the divide between the sexes whilst highlighting Sarah Jane's commitment to teaching for lesser financial rewards. Below are some of the school Log Book entries for the last three months of 1911:[40]

October 6th

W. Bryn Davies Esquire, Primary School Inspector, conducted an entrance examination for admissions to the Higher Elementary School at Pontycymer.

November 22nd

The stove has now been mended after a delay of nearly four months. Work has suffered owing to the children [catching] colds, and they had to be taken out for exercise.

December 6th

Mr Douglas Davies commenced duties this day as an un-certificated assistant at a salary of £30. He has not taught before – this being his first school.

---

[40] Brynmenyn Mixed School Log Book (1910 – 1973), formerly Ynysawdre Parish Hall School: Glamorgan Archive Services.

Christmas Approaches in 1911

THERE WERE NUMEROUS STORIES to digest in the newspapers as Christmas drew nearer. The Coronation of George V had brought colourful scenes to Westminster Abbey, whilst the Investiture of His Royal Highness Edward as Prince of Wales, in Caernarfon, had aroused interest across the country and the wider world. It was uplifting to see the nation sharing the joy of these occasions although, sadly, undercurrents of unrest were also stealing the news headlines. Whilst the volatile mining disputes in the local Rhondda Valleys had by now been resolved, the main issues across the country involved disgruntled workforces, high unemployment levels and the inconvenience of transport strikes. However, of even more concern was the fact that Britain had to keep pace with an European arms race. Winston Churchill, as First Lord of the Admiralty, was overseeing events but, unavoidably, this power-struggle was leading to war.

At Abergarw, Jenkin mustered as much help as he could find to bring the crops from the fields and safely into the stores. The long hot days of summer sunshine were special times and there was a sense of real accomplishment and relief when all had been gathered in. In reality, a successful harvest has always been a farmer's principal goal which, when completed, makes way for lesser routines to fall into place. Soon it was that time when farmers, their families, and fuller congregations filtered into church and chapel pews for an evening of thanksgiving. They would acknowledge the gifts of harvest time, and the blessings that nature had so bountifully bestowed.

At St Theodore's, Sarah Jane's preferred place of worship, the Harvest Thanksgiving Services were held on Sunday and Monday, October 8th and 9th 1911. *The Glamorgan Gazette* described the two occasions, which saw Reverend Maldwyn D. Davies M.A., of Cadoxton, Barry, preaching from the pulpit, followed by Reverend W. Austin Davies B.A., of Port Talbot the following evening. Both services were packed, many failing to gain entry, whilst the boys and girls received their own separate message from the clergy. All around the church, flowers, vegetables and sheaves of corn decorated the premises and, again, generous tithes filled the offering plates.

In school the next day, Sarah Jane was motivated for classroom duties. Being back in Brynmenyn had lifted her to new heights, and she was doing her best for everyone whilst making lessons interesting. In terms of tales from the past, *The Maid of Cefn Ydfa* was an often discussed local folklore, linked to Cwm Risca, just a few miles from Abergarw – and, although Sarah Jane never knew this, her mother's cousin would later farm both these properties mentioned. The story tells of Ann Thomas who married Anthony Maddocks, of Cwm Risca, in 1725 although, so it is understood, pining, pitifully, and seemingly dying, for her true sweetheart, Wil Hopcyn, a poet and thatcher.

When turning her attention to ancient properties, Sarah Jane would have learnt that Dunraven Estate, bought by Humphrey Wyndham Esquire of Gloucester, in 1642[41], had been visited by the Duke, Duchess and Princess of Teck in the late summer of 1888. These distinguished guests, otherwise known as Princess Mary, her husband Francis, and daughter Princess Victoria Mary – also known as May, who had more recently become the nation's well-loved Queen Mary, wife of King George V – were treated to the hospitality of Lord and Lady Dunraven. As can be expected, *The Glamorgan Gazette* of September 28th 1888 reported the story from the time the party stepped from the Paddington steam train onto the red carpet at Bridgend's packed railway station. There, horse drawn carriages awaited as did the Glamorgan Artillery Volunteers who performed a gun salute, whilst street-lining crowds sported flags and banners, amidst great excitement and warm words of welcome. Wyndham Street, Dunraven Place, Caroline Street and Nolton Street all experienced the splendour of the occasion before the Royal procession made its way to Southerndown.

For stories about current affairs, Sarah Jane could explain to her scholars about Cunard's latest flagship *RMS Lusitania,* which was making a twelve-day voyage to and from the United States, returning to Fishguard before Christmas. As it transpired, this was to be no ordinary journey by the gleaming vessel which carried a large

---

[41] Details as provided on a commemorative plaque at *The Randall Memorial*, Bridgend.

number of passengers, over 3300 bags of Christmas post and silver worth £163,000.[42] Among travelling celebrities were Lord Cecil, Lady Grenfell and the Marquess of Queensberry while boxer, Jimmy Brett, was also on board, as were Welsh miners returning to the 'Land of their Fathers.' Understandably, excitement mounted at Fishguard when the sea-beauty passed Crincoed Point, Pembrokeshire, as railway workers stoked their engine fires ready to take passengers onward to their destinations.

Nature Studies assumed importance all the year round and who could blame thoughts drifting back down the road and up the winding lane to Bryngarw, where birds and squirrels amongst a wide world of animals, insects and vegetation drew on natural forces to survive. What an interesting place, where Captain Traherne, a devoted musician, is said to have practised his piano-playing outside on the lawn. But this gentleman, and his family, and his staff of white-aproned maids and hard-working boy servants, together with the dogs, horses and the rest, were floating on top of a another world whose roots sunk into the soil. There was no better venue to consider when explaining 'The Dispersal of Seeds,' a subject that concluded nature studies for the year. Here Sarah Jane offers more of her thoughts which are the last recorded in her note book:

Seeds are that part of the plant which produce the future plant. The seeds are covered [usually] with pods,

---

[42] The *Western Mail,* of December 23rd 1911: Bridgend Library Services.

juice [or] shells, to protect them from the cold and wet. If seeds began to grow in autumn, the rains in winter would rot the shells or pods and set the young plant free before they are strong enough to stand the cold. Most seeds are therefore sown in spring when the days are warm.

As December arrived, plans were in full swing for the festive celebrations and despite the dismal weather, nothing could compare with the excitement of Christmas. This season of goodwill – when families and friends get together and hostelries order greater volumes of ales and spirits – was warming the cockles of everyone's heart. Inside the parish hall, Christmas occupied the children's thoughts. It was a time for making cards and decorations; for gift-wrapping nuts, fruits, almonds, figs and jams; for dusting-down carol sheets and singing out loud. This was good practice for candlelit church gatherings, known as Plygain services that were held in the early hours of Christmas morning, when carols were sung and *cyflaith* (a smooth toffee) was the big attraction.[43] Soon, the young scholars would be marching to school 'joyful and triumphant,' as different versions of *O Come All Ye Faithful* would be heard on the school playing field.

For Sarah Jane, the end of term would bring a welcome rest on the farm, where she and her sisters could gather under the cosy light of oil lamps to tell their stories. Gramophones were popular now, as were the great works

---

[43] Web site: www. 'Plygain' Singing: National Museum of Wales, as at June 30th 2014.

of Pyotr Tchaikovsky, such as *Swan Lake* and *The Nutcracker* – pleasing thoughts, but, more importantly there would be no rushing-off to different schools the next day. Of course, there would be the thrill of being reunited with Beatrice who, having followed her eldest sister to Clifton, was around this time beginning a period of nursing training at Gloucester Royal Infirmary. But there would still be some news to share from their favourite corner of Bristol, and this, an exclusive subject where no one else belonged.

George and Jennet had sent the girls to different schools for a reason. Katie, the second daughter who had proved to be invaluable at home and who did not want to go far away, slotted into the nearby Bridgend County Intermediate School. There, she enjoyed cookery and needlework, as well as hockey, the favourite sport of most of her sisters. Margot and Mattie, both studious and determined and destined to be headmistresses, went up the local valley for higher education at the Garw Secondary School in Pontycymmer, while Marjorie, a refined young lady, attended boarding school in Cowbridge. Their combined experiences ensured that there was a lot to talk about over the holidays when the girls congregated as a group.

Sarah Jane was counting the days to Friday December 22nd when she could clear her desk and put away her classroom books. The next day provided the last chance to buy presents and, just a short train journey away, Bridgend was promising to be quite a place. There would be no dawdling down today's Court Road for the hordes of last-minute shoppers who passed between the quaint Cottage Hospital and the elegant stonework of the Police Court, where Bridgend's regular Petty Sessions determined right from wrong.

Bridgend was full of family-run shops, many having tent-like weather awnings and, almost all, with their own hanging metal advertisements, which creaked back and forth in the swirling winds. The town was going to be alive and buzzing, full to capacity: smart-suited men with hats, women with festive costumes, couples pushing small prams with big wheels, and young lads wearing waistcoats, breeches and flat caps. And most would be carrying raincoats during these wet December days. This last shopping opportunity heralded a fanfare of activity, people all around, with horse and carts at every stop and pedestrians filling the muddy streets.

Amongst the excitement, Sarah Jane looked forward to the sight of Christmas trees and decorations, the smell of mistletoe and wine, and the unmistakable sound of carols, courtesy of a local brass band. Besides the bicycles that were propped up-right alongside the kerbs, there were more of the cheeky and charismatic little veteran cars of the day, adding dash and dare-devil to the colourful streets. Being popular and of limited supply, their expensive sale prices were indicative of considerable demand, whilst ownership was the privilege of the fortunate few. They were well advertised, too, and the following is a typical entry that appeared in the local newspapers at the time:

The Mitchell £340...
the car you ought to have, at the price you ought to pay.
The Hill-climber... silent as the foot of time.

John Grace and Son Limited, Porthcawl.[44]

Sarah Jane knew that the townsfolk had, again, made a huge effort. *Mr Hocking's Boot Shop* offered the best in winter boots and slippers; *The Shop on the Bridge* had a fine seasonal collection of gifts for men and women; whilst *Jones Brothers of Paris House* had the best selection of ties for gentlemen. *The Cigar Box* was a popular choice at this time of year, whilst *Boots*, the new store that everybody was talking about, was also catching everyone's eye. Its star was on the ascendancy, helped by generous publicity in *The Glamorgan Gazette,* where a Christmas round-up of the shops and a summary of the seasonal activities featured all the above-mentioned traders in the December news:

> 'Boots!' Who has not heard of them? Recently this ambitious firm opened a shop in Caroline Street, and without doubt it is one of the most splendidly equipped in the town, the illumination of the premises at night time being a feature. The 'Cash Chemists' assure patrons of being supplied with the purest at the lowest possible rate of profit. From their stock can be purchased excellent Christmas presents.

The onset of Christmas this season, 1911, was described in the local papers as being busier than in earlier years. The railway station, for instance, saw a constant flow of trade,

---

[44]   *The Glamorgan Gazette,* of December 15th 1911: Bridgend Library Services.

its ticket-office buzzing with commuters and passengers boarding excursions into England. Equally, the post masters and mistresses were tested to the full, busily placing parcels and letters into longing, clutching hands. Everywhere red-hot fires burnt brightly, like those at Bridgend Cottage Hospital, where holly and bright berries coloured the wards, whilst festive spirits seeped between the sheets of every bed-bound heart.

Down the road in the Workhouse and the Infirmary, inmates were looking forward to the smell of their favourite beef joint as it emerged from the oven to be carved by a queue of willing and excited hands. Everyone softened to the thought of the day's easy atmosphere, and the Christmas dinner feast, washed down by helpings of warm fruit pudding – all so worthy of the wait, as were the tarts, pies and cakes that followed. Entertained by the Guardians whose joy was to see happiness emerging from the saddened eyes of familiar faces, those in abode did not disappoint, especially when gifts of tobacco, sweets and bonbons were distributed with an afternoon tea.

Sarah Jane would have read about these annual fun-filled days at the Workhouse that ended with a concert by local artists. This is when inmates were encouraged to take part, often accompanied by visiting clergy. Likewise, she recognised the part played by *Messrs Thompson and Shackell*, whose shop at the top of Wyndham Street sold pianos and musical instruments. In customary manner, this family firm would soon be pitching one of their pianos onto the back of a horse-drawn trade cart to be taken to the event, another act of charity given to a town whose own Boxing Day Eisteddfod – this year at the English Congregational Church – attracted talented singers from miles around.

Meanwhile, there was already singing and celebrating at the cottage homes in Merthyr Mawr Road where pauper-children in accommodation eagerly awaited their favourite day. Well organised by the superintendent and foster mothers, a fine spread of food had been arranged with gifts of toys and oranges for the excited girls and boys. This was no different from the seasonal goodwill that lit-up the Angelton Asylum on the outskirts of the town and the separate Parc Gwyllt premises, both respected caring institutions within the community. Quite clearly, the festive season of 1911 was proving to be a time of peace, harmony and goodwill for one and all. As for Sarah Jane, this December, more so than in previous years, was promising to deliver her best Christmas, and she could not wait for her school holidays to begin.

Disaster Strikes

I N THE RUN-UP TO CHRISTMAS, there had been severe
rainfall over the whole of South Wales as well as across
Great Britain. At home in Abergarw, Jenkin had seen the
lower fields flooded whilst the levels of the three rivers at
Brynmenyn, the Ogmore, Garw and Llynfi, had risen
considerably. Of course, their greater weight added
momentum to the flow and consequently pace whilst, all
around the hillsides, water continued to run into the
smaller tributaries. After days of torrential downpours, the
rivers were raging with power and pace as well as an
unusual sense of menace and danger.

In the *Western Mail*, these severe circumstances occupied
the news columns and striking photographs served to
illustrate the damage that had been done, under the heading
'More Views of the Disastrous Floods in South Wales.'
Alongside, were the stories, each just a few words but
endorsing the sense of chaos and devastation that had changed
the complexion of Wales' rivers and waterways, including
many within the vicinity of Bridgend. At Ystradgynlais, there
was a picture of a bridge that had been 'washed away by the
swollen river' and at Trehafod a gaping hole had been caused
by the floods.

In the *South Wales Daily News*, there are many more
revealing photographs. At Glyncorrwg, less than ten miles

from Brynmenyn, a picture shows the remains of houses whose structures had been partly washed away and, at Glyn-Neath, a steam train had been photographed wading into a sea of water at the railway station. In the next village there were 'barrels of biscuits, and other goods, floating about the yard of a store at Resolven.' Then, giving a sense of perspective to the upheaval in Ystradgynlais, a man stood 'up to his waist in water,' this being not many miles from Brynmenyn as measured by the flight of a bird. At a time when boats, moored in the principality's harbours took a battering, the news across the nation was no better: the east coast of Britain, for instance, had been hit by storms around Deal in Kent.

Meanwhile, at Ynysawdre Parish Hall, Brynmenyn's little school went ahead as usual: everybody being used to wrapping-up in warm clothes for their morning walk to lessons, when wet feet and boots were dried in front of the friendly stove that was now working well. But the rainfall simply had to ease and, at long last, Tuesday December 19th delivered fine, even sunny weather, just three days before the end of term. As stated in *The Glamorgan Gazette*, when the children arrived for school that morning, they started playing in the Ynysawdre field near the school building, which had become their playground since the previous May. Soon, everyone would move towards the hall, gathering for a day of Christmas term merriment, as part of the wind-down to the year's most special day.

Suddenly, like a flash of lightening, everybody's world was turned upside down as tragedy and horror engulfed this

Welsh community. As one of the boys near to the river bridge walked towards the school carrying a football under his arm, another knocked it from his grasp, causing the ball to roll away into the river. In an instant young Bertram Gubbins, aged nine, but known to everyone as Bertie, gave chase, determined not to lose sight of the ball. Seconds later, Bertie was seen struggling for his life in the wild waters of the Llynfi river. As Sarah Jane was called to the scene, wearing a full winter woollen skirt down to her ankles, she was next into the fast-flowing torrent, without fear or regard for the consequences, determined to save young Bertie so that they would both emerge from the water alive.

In one mad scramble for survival, both were sent downstream by the current. To everyone's relief, Bertie emerged at the river bank where his school friends dragged him out of the water to safety, while Sarah Jane was sucked away, hopelessly out of control, as she tried everything she knew to safeguard her own passage in such extreme conditions. Being cruelly disadvantaged by the weight of her heavy clothing and the unforgiving powers of the flow, her plight soon worsened as she became engaged in a frantic fight for her own life. But her efforts were in vain and, having struck her head on a rock or boulder on the river floor, she was found quite a way downstream, lying on an island of smaller stones and perfectly still.

In the chase that consumed everyone from the moment that Bertie entered the water, Headmaster Mr Thomas Johns, and his staff had been summoned for help, as well as the village police officer and local general practitioner, Dr John Thomas of Woodside. Mr Davies, the newly appointed assistant teacher in only his second week at the school, had been amongst the first to reach Sarah Jane. Every conceivable effort was made to save her life, but this was an incident of catastrophic proportions. In the space of minutes, Brynmenyn was gripped by hopelessness and cruelly robbed of a promising young teacher, who was adored by her pupils, who was lovingly awaited at home by her family, and who was a popular and happy member of the community. In Bryncethin, Llangeinor and the surrounding schools, Sarah Jane's drowning was received with disbelief, and recorded with utmost sympathy in the respective Log Books. Meanwhile, at Brynmenyn's small school in Ynysawdre, just a few simple words were enough to describe this incident, the saddest of events:

December 19th

Miss Sarah Jane Howell at this school lost her life in the River Llynfi in a heroic attempt to save a little boy – Bertie Gubbins, who had entered the water to reach a football. The boy was saved. The School did not meet for the afternoon session.

Up the road in Abergarw farm, George and Jennet were planning the big move to their new residence, Abergarw House, scheduled for the New Year. In the midst of their preparations and hopes and aspirations, Reverend J.C. Evans, now of Brynmenyn, but previously of Gilfach Goch, arrived at their door to explain what had happened. In his years in the ministry, this gentleman had been introduced to crowds of people and to almost every situation. Having conducted many funeral services, he understood how sadness penetrates so deeply, beyond hurt and pain to emptiness and hopelessness. He knew that absorbing the shock, handling the truth, and adjusting to the loss, at a time when memories flooded the system, is a personal battle of huge proportions and extreme delicacy. In a report that appeared in the *South Wales Daily News* dated December 23rd 1911, this local minister, more than 70 years of age, admitted that...

> never in his life had he so hard a task to perform as when he broke the news of the tragedy to the sorrow-stricken parents.

That morning, Sarah Jane's sisters were in school, apart from Katie, who was now a seamstress at *Miss Stuchbery's*, a high class dress shop for ladies in the middle of Bridgend. In the top floor of the spacious premises at Caroline Street whilst at work, her concentration was broken when the lady proprietor delivered the urgent message from her mother that she was wanted at home. Putting down her materials at once, Katie returned to Abergarw, where her parents and neighbours had gathered in the back of the house, broken-hearted and grief-stricken. Experiencing the gloom, eeriness and weeping-wails upon walking through the front door, Katie saw her sister, her bosom pal and best friend, lying soaking-wet, but peacefully at rest. She had a gash on her forehead, and was most certainly dead.

The Inquest

IN THE AFTERNOON of Thursday December 21st, two days after the unthinkable, the inquest took place at Betharan Chapel, with Mr W.A. Williams, deputy coroner, presiding over formalities alongside Reverend Eynon Lewis, who was the foreman. The next day, *The Glamorgan Gazette* gave a full account of events, which saw George Howell breaking down in tears as he was called to take an oath. He described his daughter as being 'of a fearless disposition.'

Charles Headon, one of the school boys, aged fourteen, had witnessed the ball in the river as well as Bertie Gubbins swiftly giving chase. In Charles Headon's recollection, his teacher, Sarah Jane, called for Bertie to come away from the water. But in no time, he was immersed and was being swept downstream. By the time Charles Headon had rushed to the riverside with another boy to help Bertie, he could see his teacher...

> coming down the river trying to swim on her back. She
> never reached the boy. The boys held out a stick to her,
> and she failed to catch it.

As Sarah Jane was fast disappearing out of sight, this same witness called another pupil to run and fetch the teachers, with Mr Johns, the headmaster, quick to arrive. Soon Mr Douglas Davies, the new assistant, was racing to her assistance along the riverside path as Charles Headon set-off in search of a police officer. At this point, he again caught sight of Sarah Jane ...

> in the middle of the river. She had stopped on some stones... Mr Davies, myself and some of the assistants then got her out. She was not then alive.

At 9.30 am, Dr John Thomas, Woodside, reported for duty, immediately noticing a number of people trying to resuscitate Sarah Jane. He saw a swelling on her forehead, which was the likely cause of a quick loss of consciousness. When the doctor arrived, he had every expectation of reviving Sarah Jane, but this was not possible. He stated that at the spot where Bertie had braved the fast flow there was a natural 'walk into the river,' but at the scene 'where Miss Howell entered there was a sharp slope into deep water, with large boulders at the bottom.' Dr Thomas' understanding was that 'she had fallen and struck her head on one of the boulders.'

In seeking to clarify the facts, the coroner turned to the young scholar, Charles Headon:

> 'As you were going to the school, you say you saw the ball going into the river, and Gubbins tried to save it. Did he fall in?'
> 'Yes.'
> 'How did Miss Howell get on her back? Had she fallen?'
> 'I don't know, sir. I was trying to get Bertie Gubbins.'
> 'Did he get ashore by himself?'
> 'Yes sir.'
> 'You don't know whether Miss Howell tried to swim or fell in?'
> 'No.'

At this precise point the foreman sought additional explanations from the witness:

> 'Were Miss Howell and Bertie Gubbins by the side of
> the river before you got there?'
> 'No.'
> 'How did the ball get into the river?'
> 'Bertie Gubbins knocked it out of another boy's hand
> and went after it.'
> 'Was it after Bertie got to the side [that] you saw
> Miss Howell?'
> 'Yes. He had gone down several times; then I saw
> Miss Howell.'
> 'Could Miss Howell swim?'
> 'No.'

When Mr Douglas Davies was called to make a statement, he explained that Charles Headon was on the opposite bank and it was this same pupil who directed him to the place where Sarah Jane lay:

> It was about a quarter of a mile lower down the river.

As all eyes fixed upon the coroner, no one could envy the officer's role in having to search for the painful facts so soon after a tragedy of such proportions. His task was to divorce himself from the emotional charge that filled the room, so as to capture the key issues – Bertie's youthful endeavour, Sarah Jane's bravery and fortitude, and the river's raging severity. Whilst, upon questioning, the outcome no doubt appeared as clear as crystal to his trained senses and intuition, what also emerged from the story was a reminder of how thin the dividing line is between safety and danger; success and failure; triumph and disaster – indeed life and death. In his mind he had assembled the given facts into the most innocent of pictures: children and teachers walking happily to school near the end of Christmas term. Yet it took a mere blip to alter completely the course of events. It was as if this image had been mounted on a china plate, and the slightest slip had caused it to fall to the floor and be broken into pieces. It was another extraordinary example of life's uncertainties and, throughout all, Sarah Jane's bravery shone through.

As this gentleman, the coroner, concluded events, he praised Charles Headon for his performance, whilst confirming Sarah Jane's ending amounted to 'Accidental Death by Drowning.' Then he made it clear that in his opinion the essential basics of First Aid in schools should be taught to senior pupils and staff as carried out by the Red Cross or Ambulance members. He would be making his personal recommendations to the Local Education Authority in this respect.

Reverend Eynon Lewis was next to speak, mentioning that 'the young lady had sacrificed her life to save another,' He believed that Sarah Jane's heroism should be recognised by the Royal Humane Society, whilst also expressing his belief that if a fund was to be started for an official memorial, public support would be considerable.

At this point, the coroner offered his personal respect to Sarah Jane for her bravery in sacrificing so much to save another person's life: 'Everyone's sympathy would go out to the relatives of one who had the moral and physical courage to do that,' he stated.

The headmaster, Mr Johns, was not present at the Inquest, although he had immediately reported to the riverside when the incident occurred. When earlier interviewed he shed light on the location where his selfless young assistant had been found at...

> a wooden bridge which crosses the river underneath the railway bridge near to the Tondu Football Field... [where] the water is shallow in the centre, an accumulation of silt having created a sort of bank in mid-stream.[45]

This was in the vicinity of Pandy Farm, near the site where the Llynfi and Ogmore rivers merge as one.

As the formal proceedings came to an end at Betharan, young Bertie Gubbins was only a short distance away at his home. Although understandably still shaken by recent events, he was being interviewed by a reporter for *The Herald* weekly newspaper. In his own words, Bertie recalled the awful incident, which would sadly live with him for the rest of his life:

> I was playing football in the field and my ball went into the river. I went in after it, but was swept off my feet. I shouted and the teacher then jumped into the water. That was the last I saw of her. I think I got out of the water without her assistance.

As regards the location of the field to which Bertie refers, Sarah Jane's sister, Margot, aged thirteen at the time, provided more details when speaking publicly about the sad

---

[45]   *The Glamorgan Gazette*, December 22nd 1911: Bridgend Library Services.

story many years later. These are her words having just explained that the school premises were at the 'roadside' between Brynmenyn and Tondu:

> The school did not have a playground, but the children were given the use of a field across the road...
>
> On her way to school, my sister noticed that the boys were playing football in the field and she went to get the boys in lines ready for school...
>
> All came along and as they were half way across the river bridge a boy from behind pushed the ball from under the arm of a boy in front...

And this is how Margot remembers the incident being received in the community:

> This tragedy cast a gloom not just in Brynmenyn but throughout the district. My sister was a well-known, likeable girl, tall, slim and full of the joys of living. This sudden end to a promising life was unbelievable.

In all the papers, Sarah Jane had been so rightly praised for her courage and selflessness. In countless articles, many of the people interviewed – including her sister, Margot – had also credited Sarah Jane for bringing Bertie safely to the river bank. We will never know the exact details, other than what has been reported, whilst the comment from Bertie's mother, Mrs Gubbins, also to *The Herald*, during this time of personal upheaval for her own family also, indicates just how difficult an act it would have been for Sarah Jane to have saved the young scholar in such severely testing circumstances:

Mrs Gubbins... explained that her son was, she understood, carried about 60 yards by the strong current.

When interviewed by a reporter for, what is believed to have been, this same newspaper,[46] Headmaster Mr Johns was asked about his former member of staff, as well as his opinion about the tragic happening. And when replying, Mr Johns was 'enthusiastic in his eulogy of the deceased teacher.' He explained that Sarah Jane was 'very much liked and quite a favourite amongst the scholars.' He considered her to be the 'most willing teacher he had ever met' and when praising her pleasing disposition, he stated that she was 'always cheery and happy.'

As regards the events leading to her drowning, Mr Johns paid respect to Bertie's earlier statement that he had found his own way to the river bank. 'The general theory,' he added, 'and the probable theory of the sad affair, is that on jumping into the river the young lady, becoming heavily handicapped by her garments clinging to her limbs and probably preventing any movement by her, was thrown forward by the strong current and carried away.'

Appearing to share a similar point of view, the author of an unidentified newspaper cutting that has been sealed inside Sarah Jane's Pupil Teacher's Note Book, states that when 'attracted by the cries' of Bertie and of his school friends, 'Miss Howell ran to the river bank, and without hesitating a moment went into the flood to save the boy.' At that moment, 'she was almost at once swept off her feet'

---

[46]   Newspaper cuttings held by Sarah Jane's family.

causing the current to carry her 'some distance down the river' where she later drowned. Meanwhile, the flood 'carried the boy to the bank and he was saved.'

But the final words must go to the *Western Mail's* reporter who concluded the paper's article of December 20th 1911 with the following summary:

> There are several conflicting rumours in the district as to exactly what occurred, as the only eye-witnesses were children whose statements are not sufficiently clear to be relied upon.
>
> There is, however, agreement on the point that Miss Howell lost her life in a plucky attempt to rescue one of her scholars.

Tears Flow in the Falling Rain

FOR GEORGE AND JENNET AND THE FAMILY, there was little to be gained from delaying the inevitable and this meant that Sarah Jane's funeral was arranged for Friday December 22nd, the last day of term. This allowed teachers and pupils to finish their schooling in the morning, so that everyone was free to attend the afternoon service at Betharan Chapel. It was a crowded occasion with most of the villagers in attendance, besides many other mourners from different walks of the community. Once again, all details featured fully one week later in *The Glamorgan Gazette* of Friday December 29th 1911.

Following a small private service at the farmhouse, the funeral cortege left Abergarw with the singing of *Yn y dyfroedd mawr a'r tonnau* (In the deep and mighty waters) as more rain continued to pour from the blackened skies. The choice of hymn was inspirational for the words reassuringly take away the fear of death, providing hope, lasting comfort and security, rather like an anchor in life's great oceans. As Sarah Jane's coffin was carried on 'a bier' the family moved slowly towards the village, followed by the adoring children of Brynmenyn who had come to honour their teacher, Miss Howell. They passed Abergarw House, Sarah Jane's intended new home where, as the eldest daughter, she was meant to choose her own bedroom. Alongside, George's three stone houses stood in solemn silence, where Sarah Jane once played as a little girl when they were being built. A few hundred yards away, everyone crossed the small bridge over the muddy-brown waters of the Garw river. Then, having cleared the railway line between the station gates, as well as passing the Fox and Hounds, Betharan Chapel came into full view.

For George and Jennet, Betharan, had been a peaceful and uplifting retreat over the years, as it had been for earlier generations of the Morgan family. At this fine, yet modest, building they had participated in some memorable occasions: weddings, concerts, parish teas, harvest suppers and carol services, yet the usual happiness of Christmas was this day swept, literally, worlds away. They had seen the girls enjoying Sunday school as well as choir singing and parties, and Sarah Jane had always led the way for her sisters, not only at Betharan but in all walks of life.

Inside the chapel, Sarah Jane's coffin, covered with beautiful bouquets and floral wreaths, occupied the Deacon's pew. Betharan was, as expected, bursting at the seams, with many mourners being too late to enter, and having to listen to the service dripping-wet outside. In the front seats, the family sat together, everyone consoling each other, sharing a sense of grief known to them alone. As the service got underway, conducted by three ministers, Reverend William Saunders, of Pontycymmer, Reverend Eynon Lewis, and Reverend J.C. Evans, mention was made of the countless tributes that had poured into the village from across the principality. Reverend Saunders described

Sarah Jane as 'an inspiration to the maidens of Wales,' while Reverend Eynon Lewis, a friend of Sarah Jane's family since she was a child, got up to speak.

It could not have been easy for this gentleman, a pillar of society, who not only served the local people conscientiously but did so with a friendly, common touch. He would have recalled the funeral of Evan, Sarah Jane's grandfather who, when aged seventy six, had been buried at this same venue thirteen years earlier.[47] That had been a sad occasion, but not entirely unexpected and it lacked the surreal nature of this day's gathering. Reverend Eynon Lewis had grown to respect Sarah Jane through her family connection and her teaching days in the local schools. In the midst of such sorrowful scenes he, too, was deeply saddened, having felt the full force of this unexpected blow: one severe enough, heavy enough, and cruel enough to silence a community. His tribute was deliberately short but, none-the-less touching. It emphasised that Sarah Jane was a giver in life from start to finish and who could ask for more:

> The late Miss Howell attended the Band of Hope meetings almost as soon as she could walk. She was always an unselfish little girl, and she grew up to be an unselfish woman.

He then read aloud some of the messages of kindness that had earlier been referred to. They included words from Mr T.M. Franklin, in his position as Clerk to the Glamorgan County Council, as well as from professional

---

[47] Details held inside Sarah Jane's Pupil Teacher's Note Book.

teaching bodies within Glamorganshire. Then, whilst everyone present listened to his words, Reverend Eynon Lewis took the opportunity of reminding the congregation that the Right Honourable Lord Aberdare of Duffryn House had become personally involved in raising money for a monument in memory of their sadly departed friend. He thanked everyone for their sympathy and support on behalf of the Howell family, who were in favour of a public memorial. When he next asked those present to indicate their approval to Lord Aberdare's leadership and intentions in this respect, he took great personal delight in observing a fully favourable response, which he later relayed to his Lordship with both duty and pride and without delay.

As the funeral service moved to a close the congregation rose to sing the final hymn which describes the special peacefulness that lies, invitingly, in heaven. Again, George and Jennet had chosen well; its eight verses make it a study in its own right, but here are just a few lines that were sung that day:

> Gwel, uwchlaw cymylau amser,
> O fy enaid, gwêl y tir;
> Lle mae'r awel fyth yn dyner,
> Lle mae'r ŵybren fyth yn glir
> Hapus dyrfa
> Sydd yn nofio yn ei hedd…

When translated the words mean:

> See beyond the clouds of time,
> Oh my soul, look at this expanse;
> A place where the breeze will be gentle,
> A place where the sky will be clear
> A happy multitude
> Floating in peacefulness ...

As Sarah Jane's coffin was carried outside, the rain continued to fall from the heavy clouds. There was no gushing down-pour, just a soothing, persistent fall that descended upon this sorrowful scene. At her resting place, in a part of the graveyard where previous members of the Howell family had been buried, the Reverend T.B. Phillips, of nearby Tylagwyn Baptist Church, Llangeinor, said a prayer, before more peaceful words were sung from another popular hymn. Here, again are lines taken from the first verse, followed by the translated words:

> Bydd myrdd o ryfeddodau
> Ar doriad bore wawr,
> Pan ddelo plant y tonnau
> Yn iach o'r cystudd mawr ...

These words are so meaningful in relation to Sarah Jane's drowning...

> There will be a myriad of wonders
> At the breaking of the morning's dawn
> When the children of the waves arrive
> In health and free of grief...

Of all the people who paid their last respects, there was no one better to describe this touching scene than *The Glamorgan Gazette* reporter who was present. These are some of his words:

> With a last lingering look into the grave, the mourners turned sorrowfully away, leaving a Welsh heroine peacefully sleeping beneath the weeping winter skies, leaving behind her the fragrant memory of an inspiring self-sacrifice.

No one could miss the beautiful collection of wreaths which had come from all corners of the county and beyond. Of particular importance was the one from Bertie Gubbins – still at home, unwell, after his ordeal, quoting from the Book of John in the *New Testament*[48] 'Greater Love hath no man than this that he lay down his life for his friend.' Another, from the little school at Ynysawdre Parish Hall, was also worthy of mention; it was in the form of 'a harp with broken strings.'[49] But two more interesting floral tributes had come from further afield, from two ladies who were mentioned earlier in the story. One was from *Mrs* Hobbs, of Clifton, who is thought to have been Beatrice's headmistress, whilst another, 'a plain bay, the garland of heroes' had arrived from *Miss* Hobbs, also of Clifton. This lady was Sarah Jane's principal some six or

---

[48] The Book of John: chapter 15, verse 13.

[49] Log Book entry of Bridgend Mixed School (1910 – 1973), formerly Ynysawdre Parish Hall School, December 22nd 1911: Glamorgan Archive Services.

seven years earlier, in the fulfilling days of her boarding school. Her simple message stated...

'In Memory of a Brave Woman.'

Lord Aberdare's Memorial Fund

THERE WAS NO TIME like the present for both Reverend Eynon Lewis and Lord Aberdare. Although this was Christmas time 1911, letters had already been despatched to all the leading newspapers in the country, within days of the occurrence of the drowning. Now, these busy gentlemen were attending to details of the memorial fund collection, enthused by the idea of local committees arranging collections within the Bridgend districts. These are some of his Lordship's words when replying to Reverend Eynon Lewis by letter, as published in *The Glamorgan Gazette* of Friday December 29th 1911:

> Will you tell the family and the members of your congregation how touched I am by their message to me. I cannot think that Miss Howell's life was wasted. Her name will always be remembered with pride by her fellow-teachers, and her example of self-sacrifice will stimulate and encourage generations to come.

> Yours faithfully, Aberdare.

In contacting Lord Aberdare, Reverend Eynon Lewis had played his smartest card. As the oldest son of the distinguished Henry Austin Bruce – First Baron Aberdare and Home Secretary in William Gladstone's Liberal Government[50] – Henry Campbell Bruce was himself an eminent figure as Justice of the Peace for both Hampshire and Glamorgan, and Deputy Lieutenant for his own county. Born in Duffryn House and educated in Rugby and Berlin, he became Honorary Colonel of the 3rd Voluntary Battalion of the Welsh Regiment, and it is this gentleman who took an interest in Sarah Jane's story, whilst performing a long list of other official public engagements. Some of these included being a member of the Board of Great Ormond Street Hospital London, and St John's Foundation School[51] and although his offices were demanding, they did not cause him to waver from a commitment to the Howell family in respect of the memorial collection. This is how Lord Aberdare had earlier broken the news to the press; it is a brief extract from his fuller message that was found in records kept by the Howell family:

> An act of such sublime self-sacrifice and courage deserves recognition from the whole community. I propose asking for subscriptions throughout the county to raise a simple memorial on the spot and should more money come in than is necessary, to apply it to some educational purpose in memory of Sarah Jane Howell.

---

[50]   *Oxford Dictionary of National Biography*, Volume VIII in association with 'The British Academy:' Oxford University Press: Carmarthen Library Services.

[51]   *Glamorganshire at the Opening of the (20th) Century*, Contemporary Biographies, by J. Austin Jenkins (Publishers W.T. Pike & Co., 19 Grand Parade, Brighton, 1907): Glamorgan Archive Services.

For George and Jennet, it was reassuring to realise that a man of such distinction was giving his time so generously. Sarah Jane's story had captured everyone's heart and, in the family's sadness, this gave them comfort. Of course, *The Glamorgan Gazette* continued to report every aspect of the story with not a stone being left unturned, such was the thoroughness of this newspaper and the popularity of Sarah Jane, who was now revered across the nation as *A Welsh Heroine* (Yr Arwres Cymraes).

Only a week into the New Year, a gathering of people had met to put a central committee in place, supported by the local council and various teachers' associations. Lord Aberdare was appointed as the President; Mr E.F. Lynch-Blosse, Chairman, and Reverend W. Saunders, Treasurer.[52] Reverend Eynon Lewis assumed the responsibility of the coordinating secretary, and his efforts never ceased, now setting up a network of small sub committees across the community. In Brynmenyn, there were three district committees; in Bryncethin, four; in Aberkenfig, eight, and so this trend continued to Tondu, Bettws, Coytrahen and to the villages all around. Likewise, collections and generous offerings came from all walks of the community including the care homes at Angelton and Parc Gwyllt.

In the weeks that followed, Reverend Eynon Lewis' thoughts turned to a remembrance service for Sarah Jane at Betharan Chapel. Likewise, at St Theodore's Church in Bryncethin, a similar service took place. On the latest

---

[52] *The Glamorgan Gazette* of January 19th 1912: Bridgend Library Services.

occasion, the preacher reminded everyone about Sarah Jane's involvement with their place of worship, where she was a chorister and served the Sunday school as both teacher and organist. Sarah Jane had attended the last evening service before her tragic end, and was said to be 'still in existence, but in a higher and better state.'[53] The congregation present knew that the minister was referring to her 'Spirit.' Of course, Bible and Scripture readings had taught Sarah Jane where to go in search of uplifting words such as the following, found in the Book of Galatians[54] in the *New Testament*:

> But the fruit of the Spirit is love, joy, peace, patience, kindness, goodness, faithfulness, gentleness and self-control. Against such things there is no law.

It is something of a coincidence that only a few weeks earlier, on December 27th 1911, *The Clifton Chronicle and Directory* gave an account of another teacher who had jumped into a river to save a child's life. This made headlines under the title 'Reward for Bravery' and, again, underlined the severity of the December rainfall. But the event, which took place in the vicinity of Sarah Jane's earlier schooling in Clifton and also at the same time as her drowning, ended on a different note. The teacher lived to tell the tale, and enjoyed the honour of being rewarded by officers of the Royal Humane Society who recognised life-saving achievements and acts of bravery.

---

[53] *The Glamorgan Gazette*, January 12th 1912: Bridgend Library Services.
[54] The Book of Galatians, chapter 6, verse 22.

To receive this same award on behalf of Sarah Jane was another comfort for George and Jennet: directly attributable to their caring minister. Indeed, Reverend Eynon Lewis also wrote to the Carnegie Hero Fund Trust who, likewise, responded with a much-coveted medallion in Sarah Jane's memory. There was no end to the minister's deeds, for he was writing next to Sir Goscombe John, one of Wales' most famous sculptors, who having been recognised by the Royal Academy of Arts had by now dedicated years of service to memorial monuments and Gothic designs. Meanwhile, Reverend Eynon Lewis encouraged financial contributions to keep flowing into the memorial fund from far and wide.

Among the donations, letters and tributes that arrived from distant parts was a message from the Welsh Department of the Board of Education in Whitehall. Sometimes, there were poems too, and they made interesting reading in the weekly newspapers. One such work, written by Mr Edward Williams of Gellifaelog, Dowlais, which was found among more family records, reflects the hours of dedication that this author gave to composing his verses. After explaining at the beginning of his work that Sarah Jane extended the hand of friendship to the little boy, here are some of his following lines:

'T was the hand of one who laboured,
With a motive that was high,
In the church and in the village
In the school that stood nearby.

'T was was the hand of one whose nature
Was as true as it was kind;
'T was the hand of one who loved him
For his soul as well as mind.

With a spirit like the Master's
She went forth the lad to save,
Love o'er flowing like the river
Brought her to an early grave.

Stronger than her fragile body
Was the soul that dwelt within;
Self-abandon was her glory –
Love of self was not her sin.

Mr Williams' descriptions are vivid and his message is clear: his words being amongst countless condolences extended to George and Jennet. Indeed, here was a family united as one with a community whose members shared the unique mix of sadness, incredulity, respect and pride. These next two verses highlight this special sense of pride:

And the village folk to others,
As through meadows they will roam
Will be glad to show the cottage
That she once had called her home.

They will point to yonder churchyard
Where her body is at rest
And will say in *rev'rent* whisper
'There lies one who did her best.'

It was appropriate that Mr Williams mentioned Sarah Jane's school, and how correct his words have proved to be:

> In the school among the children
> And among the teachers too,
> She in spirit will be with them
> Leading them to actions true.

And here are the last two verses of the poem, bringing Mr Williams' personal tribute to an end:

> Love like hers will live for ever,
> Live through ages yet unborn.
> Guiding those who live in darkness
> Till they see the light of dawn.

> Those who leave behind them traces
> Of a life that's noble, fine,
> Shed a fragrance through the ages
> Leading up to things divine.

George and Jennet were thrilled to receive more verses from a lady who lived on the outskirts of Bristol and whilst this person was not known to them – and it was decided not to publish her work – she had clearly met Sarah Jane during her days at Clifton. This was Mrs Bradley, mentioned, briefly, earlier in the story and described in the local paper as being from *Bitton George*. However, this was certainly meant to read *Bitton Grange*… in other words 'The Grange' residence, at Bitton, South Gloucestershire.[55]

---

[55]   *The Glamorgan Gazette*, February 9th 1912 – Bridgend Library Services.

This is an ancient property going back many centuries
and, once, the home of Jane Seymour, the third wife of
King Henry VIII.[56] It stands alongside St Mary's Church, an
imposing building, complete with spacious graveyard.
During Sarah Jane's time at boarding school, the pretty
village of Bitton was connected to Bristol and Clifton by its
own railway station about eight miles away. It is quite likely
that Sarah Jane visited this historic house – not dissimilar to
Bryngarw in Brynmenyn – on a school outing, especially as
it is known that Mrs Elizabeth Ann Bradley, who has been
traced at the property during this time, was born in
Pontypridd.[57]

Mrs Bradley was the wife of Mr Herbert Edward Bradley,
a former bank manager for the National Provincial Bank,
whose career began in Cardiff in 1883. During a twenty-year
term, he served at Chipping Sodbury and Wotton under Edge
in Gloucestershire, before taking up a senior appointment as
the manager of Brecon branch in December 1892.[58] It is there
that he served for eleven years, living for some of this time in
the nearby quiet, picturesque village of Llanspyddid.[59] In
December 1903 Mr Bradley retired, prompting a return to
the Bristol area with his family to live in Bitton at a time when
Sarah Jane was attending boarding school.

---

[56]   Web site: www.TheDowerHouse andThe Grange, Bitton.
       as at June 30th 2014.
[57]   British Census of 1911, web site: www.findmypast.co.uk
       as at June 30th 2014: Carmarthen Archive Services.
[58]   The Royal Bank of Scotland Group PLC, Archives: Edinburgh, EH12 9EG.
[59]   Local Studies Librarian, Bath Central Library.

The Beginning of
Brynmenyn's New School

A FTER ALL THE SADNESS OF 1911, regrettably, the
following year continued in similar fashion. At a time
when powerful dreadnoughts were taking to the seas,
symbolising the furious war battles that lay ahead, Titanic's
sinking on April 15th 1912 was seen as an unnecessary
disaster – not dissimilar to Sarah Jane's drowning – one that
ended beyond all doubt the false belief that certain ships
were unsinkable, whilst exposing the dangers of the new
concept 'speed.' It was only three months later when
Germany's build-up of warships continued to show no
abatement, that a young Winston Churchill put the
country's battleships on alert in the North Sea.
Understandably, this news was received with alarm and sent
shivers down spines across the country.

Throughout this landmark year in British history,
Brynmenyn's two little schools at Betharan Vestry and
Ynysawdre Parish Hall soldiered-on in the knowledge that a
brand-new building was being built at a site south of the
village Common. It was to accommodate the local children
and, from all accounts, it was going to be a fine place,
situated high above the road leading into the village from
Tondu. Only a short walk away was the railway station,

sitting at the fork-junction of two important rail routes and, as ever, directing the steam trains back and forth. From the school, the railway platform and stationmaster's house, with decorative potted plants and evergreens, would be seen under clouds of steam blown into the air, whilst the sharp and regular blasts of the trains' whistles determined the passing hours and minutes, rather like Mr Beha's watches at his high class shop in Dunraven Place, Bridgend. But, taking one day at a time, it was 'business as usual' for both Brynmenyn's temporary schools. This meant more entries appearing daily in the Log Books, such as the following extracts that were recorded by the Infants School[60] before leaving Betharan:

> *March 29th 1912*
> His Majesty's Inspector's Report:
> There is very little room for games inside the building,
> but as much movement as possible is allowed out of
> doors, and the children look bright and happy.
> The work is nicely correlated and the performance of
> the Senior Division (Standard I) is highly credible,
> showing careful and intelligent preparation, not only in
> that class, but in the classes below.

> *June 12th 1912 ...*
> School closed for half day, granted by managers in
> consequence of a fete at Coytrahen.

---

[60]   Brynmenyn Council Infants School 1909 –1912:
Glamorgan Archive Services.

July 7th 1912 ...

Very low attendance: due to children's carnival in the district.

December 20th ...

School closed for Christmas Holiday – (until) January 6th 1913.

There was excitement all around the village when the move took place to the new school a week later on Monday January 13th and, better still, the children were sent home early because some furniture had not been transferred from the former premises. Two days later, there were more celebrations when the official opening arrived. This was, according to the Log Book[61] a 'Red Letter Day in the history of the school.' It was a time for teachers and children to come together, putting behind them past events for a fresh start. That morning, the scholars were given tasks to perform in readiness for the official ceremony in the Central Hall, as the day's records reveal:

> At two o'clock in the afternoon, Councillor David Thomas, one of the managers of the Ogmore Group of Schools, declared the new school open – being presented with a gold key by Mr Pulsford on behalf of Knox and Wells, Contractors, Cardiff.

For everyone, this news was a breath of fresh air, away from concerns of an ever-nearing war and sad news of Titanic's compelling story that continued to reveal fresh news months

---

[61] Brynmenyn Council School Mixed (1910 – 1973):
Glamorgan Archive Services.

after the event. At a time when modern schools were appearing in different parts of the locality, most people recognised that Brynmenyn's new establishment was following almost directly in the wake of a similar new set-up in Llangan, just into the Vale of Glamorgan, some six or seven miles away. By coincidence, Llangan's new council school had also taken over the functions of two smaller concerns that had served its own popular rural community for generations – in fact, ever since well-intentioned estate owners put in place education for the local children.

Radcliffe School was no more than a one-room class, complete with a stove, smoking chimney, and outside weathercock. Penllyn was much the same, a humble base where children could learn in the warmth and shelter when, outside, it was bucketing-down with rain. Nevertheless, both schools provided essential paving stones to give youngsters a start in life. They had their own stories, too, just like other schools of this era, some of whom prepared their own ink, either from berries or from the remains of the bark of dead trees. To do this, teachers and pupils mixed the materials with water carried up from the streams, usually by the masters, one or two earthenware pots at a time. Life was simple then, and slow: 'Come day, go day, and God sent Sunday,' is the old adage and how true but, that apart, ideals and goals were just as high, despite forever having to scrape the bottom of the barrel of resources.

Now, a year later, it was Brynmenyn's turn and comprehensive coverage of the opening ceremony of the new school appeared in *The Glamorgan Gazette* of Friday January 24th

1913. There was a large crowd that mid-winter's day, all thrilled to see Brynmenyn stepping into the limelight with such fine premises. Catering for 214 children, with generously-sized classrooms, conveniences, hall and playground area, it would be raising the village's profile, and little expense had been spared, so it seemed. The work had been completed for the sum of £3665 on a piece of land 'one acre in extent, purchased from the Duchy of Lancaster and the Commoners, at a cost of £210.'

Here was a building to stand the test of time whose local stone was complimented by Forest of Dean bricks and trimmings; slates from the North Wales quarries; wooden block flooring in the hall and classrooms; modern tiles along the passageways; the latest in chimney fittings, and ventilation throughout. It was in every respect the model school of its day and it would also serve as the most appropriate home for the memorial, once completed, in honour of Sarah Jane.

At its main Central Hall, high-ceilinged and spacious, everyone retired for the official speeches: Mr T.E. Lewis of Blaengarw, one of the school managers, being the first to take to the floor, followed by Mr Evan Evans who offered his full thanks to representatives of the County Education Committee and the local group of school managers. This gentleman then stressed the importance of village children being provided with the same standards of schooling and staffing as the more populated areas, whilst making his concerns abundantly clear about infants less than five years of age still being left out at Brynmenyn, contrary to trends elsewhere.

The next speaker was Alderman Llewellyn who raised the subject of combating absenteeism despite primary education being free. He stressed the need for the children to attend classes, so as not to lose out in later life. Then Alderman Llewellyn touched upon the financial implications of raising the head-count, which would boost the school's entitlement to grants. Reverend W. Saunders, taking his turn to address the audience, believed that the Welsh language should play a greater part in the principality's schools without delay, and he made his views clear:

> Why could they not have Welsh? (Applause). The morality and religion of their country depended on their keeping the Welsh language alive. (Loud applause)

At this stage, an amusing incident took place when two of the managers of the same School Board voiced their differing opinions about the attitude of modern-day pupils. Mr T. Williams, Chairman, had been disappointed by a decline in the standard of children's behaviour – only to be shot down by the next speaker, his colleague, Mr Job Baker. Amidst loud laughter in the room, Mr Baker entertained everyone when giving his point of view:

> It was quite true that they did not bow and scrape to the parson or the policeman today… In the old days they did; well if they didn't they would 'get it' when they got to school [!]

The newspaper article described the tea and refreshments that followed, as well as the singing of the pupils which ended the formalities of the day. This confirmed that

Brynmenyn School had arrived and would provide well for the children of the village long into the future. More importantly for George and Jennet Howell, they knew from their association with the current teachers and managers that the memories of December 19th 1911 would continue to be respected, and that their daughter would live on in the thoughts and minds of everyone connected with this new prestigious school.

The Reflections of a Farmer's 'Boy'
and the Sarah Jane Howell Award

E VER SINCE the Howell family moved across the road to Abergarw House, life on the farm, and particularly in the farmhouse, was a lot quieter. But nothing altered Jenkin's habit of a lifetime in rising early to take hay and feed to the animals in the cold winter mornings, sometimes with a thick head from a visit to the Miller's Arms the night before. Jenkin was by now married to the love of his life, Mary Thomas of Pantynawel farm, Llangeinor, whose support ensured that farm life ticked along quietly. Better still, there was another pair of helping hands at Abergarw, belonging to sixteen year old Rachael Ann Webb, who had been posted there following her application to join the Woman's Land Army. As a dreaded war appeared more likely, putting the shipment of food supplies to Britain under threat, Rachael arrived at Abergarw during a break in her nursing training. She was just one of many young ladies who were making a difference across the country by lending their support to food production.

Rachael's experiences at Abergarw are recalled in her memoirs, *From Caerau to the Southern Cross*.[62] In a full chapter dedicated to her life on the farm, which she thoroughly

---

[62]   Alun Books of Port Talbot (1987): Bridgend Library Services.

enjoyed, she explained that her arrival coincided with the period that followed Sarah Jane's drowning. It was when the family were, in fact, packing their possessions ready for the move, making way for Rachael to occupy Sarah Jane's bedroom, and even the bed where she used to sleep. This was hardly the start that Rachael had hoped for but she soon thrived under Jenkin's direction, amongst the rough-and-tumble of old time farming.

Rachael explained that the animals had been given a name by Jenkin, an indication of his affection for them, and she learnt her milking 'trade' on poor-old Daisy, one of the more tolerant of the few dairy cows. Rachael recalled the occasion when, cleaning away muck from the cowshed one day, she burst into song with words of *The Farmer's Boy*. This immediately brought a concerned Jenkin (Mr Morgan is how she politely called him) out onto the farm yard to find out what was going on. 'He, too, started laughing,' wrote Rachael, before Jenkin responded with the words 'I can see that you are going to be better than any farmer's boy!'

Rachael described the 'doorsteps of bread,' and rhubarb puddings that she was given to eat when sitting on the wooden settle in the pantry. On one occasion, she stepped in for Mrs Morgan when taking chickens, eggs and cream to the market in Bridgend, riding 'side-saddle' on the way. After milking time, when returning the cattle to the fields, she sometimes took the direct route by walking the animals through the river. To avoid the water, she would cadge a lift from the most willing cow, which was no issue to Rachael, a dare-devil, just like most of Sarah Jane's sisters in their youth. Speaking gently into the ear of one of the herd, 'You are going to give me a piggy-back [aren't you?],' Rachael launched herself across the animal's upper midriff 'like a sack of potatoes.'

> Mr Morgan saw me coming back like this one day, riding on the cow's back, and said, 'Oh merch i, you're a caution!'… ['Oh my girl, we'll have to watch out for you'].

Rachael recalled an event that no doubt lived in the memory of them both. Having raked and dried the hay one summer's day, Jenkin was hoisting clumps high onto the gambo, one pitchfork at a time. Spreading the load on top of the pile was Rachael who, having eaten well from the food brought into the field by Mrs Morgan that day, was beginning to tire. When Jenkin called to her, 'We're finished now, *bach* (a friendly if not affectionate term),' the two horses, also feeling the effect of the day's hard labour and believing that these words were meant for them, immediately pulled away – as poor Rachael tumbled all the way down onto the bone-hard field. Of course, Jenkin, fearing the worst, could not get to Rachael quick enough, and was mightily relieved that she was not seriously hurt. But he knew that she had been shaken and, later in the night, both he and his wife took turns to check that their valuable helper was comfortable as she slept.

In another of her tales, Rachael mentioned that she and Jenkin used to make a friendly agreement at the end of the day's work. This involved Jenkin giving her a swede, which she ate by the kitchen fire, while he disappeared down to the Miller's Arms. As soon as Rachael finished the food, which Mrs Morgan peeled for her and which she chose to eat raw, it was then her duty to bring Jenkin back from the pub. If Jenkin wanted to stay longer, he conveniently brought Rachael a larger swede, so that it took her longer to eat! When Rachael peeped into the doorway of the inn, Jenkin usually looked up, saying: 'Right, merch fi,' [right, my girl], and then he followed her out. But one evening he produced a really big swede, effectively 'buying' a little more drinking time and teased her when she arrived rather earlier than expected:

'Did you eat your swede, Rachael?'
'Yes.'
'All of it?'
'Yes'
'Well, well,' he said, 'Such a little tummy, such a large swede! Where do you put it?'

There is no doubt that Rachael enjoyed her time at Abergarw farm, where she appreciated a variety of home-cooked meals besides raw swedes! But one day, she was asked by her mother to join her at Bridgend railway station when she said her goodbyes to Rachael's sister, Emily, and her young family, who were on their way to join a ship bound for Australia and a new life. Rachael recalled her mother running after the train to hear Emily's last few words, almost jumping aboard such was the emotional impulse. This parting devastated her mother and, later that night, when lying in Sarah Jane's former bed reliving the incident, Rachael was also consumed by sadness, weeping almost uncontrollably, causing Jenkin and his wife to keep vigil over her once again. Indeed, the event triggered her departure from Brynmenyn, for it was not long after this that Rachael felt obliged to return home to care for her mother. Looking back at her time on the farm, she described 'Mr and Mrs Morgan' as 'two of the nicest people' she had ever known.

It is not certain whether Rachael was replaced at Abergarw, although this is likely because women were now rallying to the country's call of duty in ever-increasing numbers. Turning their skills to factory, farming, manual and munitions work, as well as clerical, office and other duties, they were effectively jumping into the shoes of men and women who had gone overseas to fight in the battles. Of course, August 1914 ended all uncertainties about the arms race and the build-up of dreadnoughts and naval power when Germany's invasion of neutral Belgium brought Britain and its Commonwealth countries into the war. In no time, hundreds of thousands of men were signing-up for active service, before being whisked away to new training centres appearing across the country and then thrust into the bloody battles of a long and senseless conflict that continued far longer than people ever imagined.

Bridgend and Brynmenyn could not escape the hurt and the catastrophes, as letters, news and casualties made their way back to the homeland. It was a time of extreme sadness and for digging deeply to find the will and determination to carry on, hoping and praying for cessation to the fighting and the start of a new world. At such a time, comfort, no doubt, came to those who looked back on treasured moments from the past: innocent days of peacetime living which, in reality, must have seemed a world away. One such moment is recorded in the Log Book entry of March 9th 1912 for Brynmenyn Mixed School at Ynysawdre Parish Hall. It concerns the visit of His Majesty's Inspectors and captures the profound statement of a gentleman whose words have proved to be true:

> 'The School has recently passed through a severe trial in the loss of Sarah Jane Howell... Her heroic act has, however, cast a lustre on the School and cannot fail to have an inspiring effect on many generations of future scholars – especially as it is to be commemorated by a tablet or other permanent record on the wall of the new building.'

Now, more than three years later, on January 16th 1915, the memorial was, at long last, officially unveiled; and, again, we are indebted to *The Glamorgan Gazette* for providing the full story in the following week's news. Scheduled to begin at 3pm, on a day of mixed showers, Lord Aberdare, who was due to perform this task was, surprisingly, nowhere to be seen. After an hour of waiting, the small Central Committee – as well as family and friends, including Mr Davies, the school teacher who had recovered Sarah Jane's body from the river – went inside the school for a meeting. Chaired by Mr David Thomas, and supported by Reverend Eynon Lewis, Reverend W. Saunders, Alderman W. Llewellyn and Reverend Morgan Thomas of Bettws – the assembled party were also joined by Mr L.S. Merrifield, the sculptor from Chelsea, who had been recommended to perform this piece of work by Sir Goscombe John.

In every sense the school premises were looking in good order for the arrival of Lord Aberdare. In these early years the girls and boys, who had their own separate playgrounds at break time, had come together with their teachers to do some gardening alongside the flower beds. Of course, vegetable allotments were now appearing everywhere across the country for essential wartime food and most schools were busy in this respect. Lord Aberdare would have been impressed had he arrived but, for whatever reason, he was detained elsewhere and his presence was missed.

After deciding to proceed in his Lordship's absence, the small ceremony began with the singing of *O God our Help in Ages Past*. Then the Chairman, who had personally known Sarah Jane, said a few words, describing her 'smiling' and 'modest' nature. He stated that people who had seen her in the street 'would never have thought that such courage rested beneath her calm character.'

Next, Reverend Eynon Lewis explained the successful campaign to raise money for the memorial, mentioning that Lord Dunraven had initially been contacted concerning the acquisition of a piece of land for the purpose of erecting the finished work. However, it was later decided to position the memorial within the grounds of Brynmenyn School instead. Reverend Eynon Lewis then made way for Reverend Saunders, Treasurer of the local committee, to dot the 'I's, and to cross the 'T's concerning the public subscriptions received. The fund, which had been bolstered by contributions from overseas, had raised the massive sum of £214, 16s, 8d, to which interest, of two guineas, would be added. This was formidable and, even after modest administration fees, there was more than enough money to discharge the memorial cost of £105. As regards the remainder, this was to be used at a later date to arrange an annual scholarship for the children of Brynmenyn and neighbouring schools in memory of Sarah Jane.

At this stage Mr Merrifield, sculptor, paid his respect to Sarah Jane, stating, 'It had been a great pleasure to be associated with such a thoroughly brave person as Miss Howell.' Then, it was time for presentations to be made to George and Jennet. This was carried out by Alderman Llewellyn, who delivered a parchment certificate from the Royal Humane Society, as well as a medallion from the Carnegie Hero Fund Trust. Both these awards for bravery touched the hearts of George and Jennet, and they have remained within the family ever since.

Alderman Llewellyn's next duty was to remove the memorial's covering, revealing a striking bronze model, mounted upon a tall white stone column. On one side of this attractive base was another bronze plaque of Sarah Jane, encircled by an arrangement of floral design; on the other was a bronze plaque bearing the following words:

> This memorial was erected by public subscription in
> memory of the Brynmenyn heroine, Sarah Jane Howell,
> of Abergarw farm, the school teacher, who gave her life

to save one of her pupils from drowning in the Llynfi river on the 19th day of December 1911. Greater love hath no man than this that he lays down his life for his friend.

Sharing the historic moment with their parents and sisters, were Margot and Mattie Howell, who both became teachers in later life with Margot having the pleasure of serving this same school. They soon learnt about the scholarship to which Reverend Saunders had earlier referred, and would be invited back to make presentations on behalf of the family in later life. In an evening address that Margot made to an audience in Barry when she was a lot older, entitled *A Welsh Heroine*, she gave details about the Sarah Jane Howell Award granted to the pupil at Brynmenyn School who gained 'the highest marks in the Scholarship Examinations.' She also mentioned that there was further recognition granted to the best performing pupil in the Ogmore Group of Schools, which included the Garw and Gilfach valleys, as well as the district leading up to, and including, Tondu. In essence, this represented the catchment area Sarah Jane served as a teacher.

On this occasion, Margot went on to say that the presentation of awards took place following a short ceremony at Brynmenyn School each July. All the children and teachers gathered in the Central Hall, alongside guests, including the parents and family of the prize-winners, well-known dignitaries, district councillors, and representatives of the local educational board. This was an event that Margot was proud to attend and greatly enjoyed. In an extract from her speech, she explains in her own words the part she played in the proceedings:

> Whilst the children provide a pleasing musical programme, I am asked to give the history of the award, before handing-over a cheque to the boy or girl who is to receive it. This is followed by a tea for the guests and school staff and, during the following week, the school receiving the reward is given a holiday. In this way, my sister's heroism has not been forgotten.

A Brief Epilogue

AFTER SARAH JANE'S DAYS, George and Jennet and the girls settled into Abergarw House, which provided the fresh start that the family needed. This residence defined a new tomorrow and it remained within the family's ownership for most of the twentieth century. Across the road, Jenkin knew where to find help and company at all times whilst he and his wife continued to enjoy farming life. Jenkin's end came on July 22nd 1926 when he was buried at St Cein's Church at the top of Llangeinor Mountain. His grave overlooks the wild and open hills and on his headstone are the words 'Yn 69 mlwydd oed,' meaning he died aged sixty-nine.

When considering Jenkin's memories of Abergarw, it is probably a blessing that he did not see the arrival of the new roadway from Brynmenyn to Llangeinor around the late 1930s, which altered the approach to both the farm and Abergarw House. Likewise, the later demolition of the farmhouse and his working sheds in favour of today's pleasant new housing may have shocked Jenkin. Indeed, one can imagine him thinking 'Beth yn y byd sy'n digwydd nawr?' (What in the world is happening now?) – as tradition, and the past, gave way to innovation, and the future.

As regards the Howell family, Katie, now the eldest daughter, married David Edwards an engineer from

Lampeter in West Wales. Katie continued to maintain the family connection at Betharan Chapel as organist for a remarkable sixty years. She and David lived at Abergarw House for the rest of their lives and appreciated Brynmenyn's relaxed and friendly ways. Their daughter is, of course, today's Janet Moody of Whitchurch who has often been mentioned during the story.

Beatrice went on to complete her training in Gloucester before starting her own private nursing practice in Cardiff. In the course of her duties, she looked after the son of one of her clients who, suffering from an allergy at the time, was covered from head to foot in bandages. This was merchant naval officer, Captain Stanley Kempton Penn, who was attracted to Beatrice's gentle, supportive voice. When the bandages came off, he also liked her face and they were later married at St Cein's Church (Jenkin's resting place) and the reception was held at the Dunraven Hotel, Bridgend. They had two sons, Neville, a civil servant in his younger days, and George, who became a doctor. Until the age of eight, George attended Brynmenyn School and he enjoyed his time there, although he never forgot colliding, occasionally, with the school's swinging doors – and emerging second-best, complete with bleeding nose! George became a well-known general practitioner in West Wales, serving at Dolycwrt Surgery, Whitland, for 42 years, where he is still remembered with affection throughout his former practice area.

Margot and Mattie ended their days as spinsters, both being respected teachers in the locality. After enjoying many years working at Brynmenyn, Margot later became the Headmistress of Pandy School, Aberkenfig, where her friendly, quiet and conscientious manner endeared her to pupils and parents. Meanwhile Mattie took charge of Colwinston School, a pretty country set-up with a small, charming building, bell tower and playground. Mattie possessed boundless energy and worked tirelessly for the well-being and betterment of pupils, and succeeded in getting them all to do well, not only her brightest and best.

Of course discipline counted immensely, and when Mattie once had cause to reprimand a little boy, he bolted out of the classroom door, through the school entrance and down the narrow, winding lane. He ran into the countryside as fast as his legs could carry him, believing he would find refuge, but how wrong he was. Mattie, well used to chasing ponies around the fields of Abergarw, and the biggest tomboy of all the girls, gave chase, her feet pounding the dusty tracks. When she caught the boy a few miles away, there was no need for a row or even a word; he had met his match and behaved impeccably from thereon.

Interestingly, it is in this same idyllic setting that Mattie and some of her young scholars are understood to have met Agatha Christie, the famous author who was known to frequent Colwinston to visit family members. The village certainly gave Mattie her halcyon days; it is where she became valued in the community and where she could hardly put a foot wrong. But, in later years, Mattie moved to Barry to fulfil another teaching post. When she died, well into her nineties, her ashes were scattered in the graveyard of the Church of St Michael and All Angels – in Colwinston, of course.

Marjorie married David Jones, a well-known baritone and teacher. They settled in Penygraig and were both active in the community but, sadly, Marjorie died at a young age in 1933. Burying another of his daughters was a further blow for George Howell, whose own end came just two weeks later. Whilst working in the garden of Abergarw House, he paused for a rest and fell asleep, never to awake. His widow, Jennet, died three years later. She had reached her 'three-score years and ten,' just like her husband, George, and her father, Evan.

As regards young Bertie, we cannot imagine him growing older but he, like everyone else, moved on in years and in life. In the days of schooling at Ynysawdre Parish Hall, Bertie was joined by his brother, Ronald, and sisters, Dorothy and Isabella. No doubt, Bertie wandered down to the train station at Tondu to admire the steam engines because he followed his father – also named Bertie, who was an engine driver for Great Western Railway – by becoming a railway clerk.

Making contact with two of Bertie's relatives was a joy for the author at the final stages of this project. Bertie's niece, June Fairburn, and her brother, Peter Evans, who today live in England and Australia respectively, left Wales at a young age without getting to know their uncle. But, they are aware that he was fond of collecting cigarette cards in his younger days. Bertie, whose birth was registered at Oxford, settled in Swindon and lived near to the Great Western Railway centre, a major player in a town that grew directly from its railway operations.

Being immersed in the world of steam trains must have given Bertie – who once visited George and Jennet Howell when he returned to Brynmenyn – a busy life. However, it was to be short-lived, because Bertie, who married Beatrice Kingston (although known as Olive, her middle name) in the beautiful St Mark's Church in Swindon in the summer of 1932 – died at the age of forty-five. His death occurred in March 1948 when Bertie was at the Medical Fund Hospital, an establishment in his adopted town that not only tended to the medical needs of the G.W.R. staff but influenced the foundation of today's National Health Service – which, incidentally, began its operations only four months later in the summer of 1948. Bertram Thomas Alfred Gubbins, once of Brynmenyn, and always 'our Bertie,' was laid to rest at Radnor Street Cemetery in Swindon.

It was around the time of Sarah Jane's drowning that Brynmenyn had its own Mines Rescue Station. For years, coal production in South Wales remained high enough for teams of men to be engaged in dangerous life-saving duties, often accompanied by canaries whose sensitivity to gases and smells provided telling information. But, when coal demands eased and more collieries closed, this station, likewise, assumed lesser importance before ending its days in the 1980s. By now, the railway lines that travelled through Brynmenyn and up to the Garw and the Ogmore valleys had also fallen-prey to changing times, as had the smaller station stops along the way. Today the crossing gates at Brynmenyn serve as a sad reminder of a former life and an industrial past that has long gone.

If Jenkin had known that the Fox and Hounds would still be open for business, years after its heyday – the old cellars clanging with the sound of today's metal barrels – he would have raised his glass in approval. What a proud history lives within its walls, having shared countless occasions with Betharan chapel across the road, and so much railway activity at its main front entrance. Over the years its bars and function rooms shone a permanent light in the village, staging meetings and social events for the locals to enjoy for more than a century. And we must not forget that it witnessed 'The Boar's Christmas Outing' in 1897, when Jenkin strolled into town, guns blazing.

Llangeinor Arms at the top of the mountain is today as popular as ever, still doing what it knows best, just like St Cein's Church next door – both enjoying terrific views and the feeling of being on top of the world. Sadly, the same cannot be said for Betharan Chapel, which is no longer a place of worship although still a symbol of reverence in the village and a building that will serve new purposes into the future, whilst Sarah Jane's St Theodore's Church was demolished years ago. Jenkin's favourite Miller's Arms and the old water wheel nearby went the same way, as did Abergarw Brewery, which is remembered for having a tall tower and big stone wall on which its name appeared and for the Sentinel lorry deliveries to the local pubs which replaced the horse and carts.

The old road to Llangeinor remains as a narrow single track, twisting and turning as it climbs the mountain: a memory lane, passing under canopies of trees, alongside dry stone boundaries and open moorland. Who can fail to wonder what stories sit within these walls: each laid one piece upon another, row upon row of rustic-rugged ornaments, defying the wild winter winds and storms, decorating the hills and dales. For certain, the old road to Llangeinor offers an intriguing and invigorating walk and, as the newspaper reporter said way back in 1897: 'Once you get to his breezy crest, all is well with you.'

We will never tire of hearing tales of the old mining days although it is heartening to know that new life has emerged from the scene of such former enterprises. Bedford Park, set in acres of once serious iron, coal and brick production, is a typical example, and the old buildings and relics from the past are still visible among the encroaching undergrowth. So also is the Parc Slip Nature Reserve, situated on the gentle hills near Aberkenfig, serving to remind us how devastating are the consequences of underground explosions and accidents. These following words were recorded by the commemorative committee at the memorial feature dedicated to those who died at the colliery on St Mary Hill Fair day in 1892:

Our Fathers, Our Brethren, For Ever
In the explosion which occurred at about 8.30 a.m. on the 26th August 1892, 112 men and boys from this locality lost their lives. The stones which compose this monument represent these 112 victims. There were 39 survivors.

This touching tribute is one of many to be found around the hills and valleys of the old mining works near Brynmenyn, another example being the small black coal cart standing alongside the road at Lluest in the Garw valley. The courageous men of our mines will not be forgotten, some having innocently gone to work in the morning, but never to return home at night.

One might wonder if Brynmenyn's former miners found time to shoot pheasants, rooks and rabbits around the nearby fields – perhaps even with Captain Traherne and his shooting parties at Bryngarw estate. This wonderful venue, occupying centre stage in Brynmenyn's new look village, where top-spin tennis was played on its front lawns, is described as *A Hidden Treasure* within its official booklet. Indeed, Bryngarw Hotel and Country Park is more than this, for it is a piece of yesterday, coated with today's refinements.

The former site of St Mary Hill Fair, bare and desolate on a cold, blustery spring day, offers enthralling views. What scenes this location once knew, and what aspirations people must have taken to its summit intent upon seizing a little happiness from the event. Today, its rolling, rugged landscape, with crusty rock outcrops, is no different from when crowds gathered at its plateau top. Whether Sarah Jane was one of these is not known, although it is extremely likely, simply because St Mary Hill Fair was 'the place to go.' The plaque, mentioned earlier, near the entrance to the old fairground, donated some years ago by local resident, Bernard Battrick, states that the last fair at this location was in the 1950s, by which time modern trucks and transport refused to abide by the laws of narrow lanes. And, as for the two nearby hostelries, *The Bell* and *Yr Hen Dafarn*, both have undergone major refurbishments and are today private dwellings.

Over the years, Bridgend's Cottage Hospital, Workhouse and Infirmary have given way to changes, indeed a reformation and a different era, whilst certain parts of these buildings still remain. Angelton's proud establishment is today's equally important Glanrhyd Hospital, whilst its contemporary, Parc Gwyllt, closed in later years before making way for a new prison. As regards Dunraven Castle – used as a Red Cross Hospital and Convalescent home during the First and Second World Wars, respectively – this imposing landmark was taken down stone by stone and confined to distant memories and old photographs, leaving its splendid view to live on.

Sadly, the same fate befell Bridgend Town Hall. It mattered not that the Mayor's Parlour, Reading Rooms and leather bound library books brought a touch of sanctity to its inner chambers, for this landmark was also demolished, having once accommodated the Assembly Rooms, the local police constables and the county court.[63] It is all so sad, but a good reason to enjoy the words of Omar Khayyam, an eleventh-century poet:

---

[63]   *Bridgend 900* – D. Brown & Sons, Bridgend and Cowbridge, 1993 and *The Archive Photographs Series, Central Bridgend around Elder Street* compiled by Natalie Murphy in association with Bridgend Civic Trust (Chalford publishers): Bridgend Library Services.

The Moving Finger writes, and, having writ,
Moves on: nor all thy piety nor wit
Shall lure it back to cancel half a line
Nor all thy tears wash out a word of it.[64]

Bridgend has changed from the days when the small shops flourished in the packed enclosures of traditional street patterns. These are treasured memories now, just like old melodies from the bandstand concerts, and the former outdoor paddling pools, which brought soothing sobriety and a splash of excitement to the town. In 1948 recognition came with the arrival of the Royal National Eisteddfod onto Newbridge Fields: an historic occasion for Bridgend during some wet weather. Meanwhile, a mile away, Merthyr Mawr was caught under the same black clouds: an idyllic thatched hamlet on the village-green, whose nearby soft, sandy dunes once found fame in the film, *Lawrence of Arabia*.[65]

Over the water, Clifton has remained a gem of a place among Bristol's attractions and its railway station is still quaint, serving commuters as it did in Sarah Jane's days – although one of the boarding schools described earlier appears to be part of BBC-Bristol's new headquarters in Whiteladies Road. As regards both Miss Hobbs and Mrs Hobbs, they ended their days pleased to have shaped the lives of young ladies, such as Sarah Jane; indeed, this is all so evident when we consider our heroine's noble character.

---

[64] Quote by Omar Khayyam, web site: www.themovingfingerwrites, as at June 2014.

[65] Web site: www.sand dunes off the beaten track: Merthyr Mawr: as at June 30th 2014.

It is with thanks to *The Bath Chronicle* of August 5th 1922,[66] that we read of the passing of Herbert Bradley, the former bank manager who enjoyed a long retirement at Bitton Grange, and also to *The Times* who reported the death of his widow, Mrs Elizabeth Ann Bradley, fifteen-years later.[67] They left the scene in the knowledge that their three sons served in the war, with military honours being awarded to them. Sarah Jane may well have met these young men on a school outing to Bitton, and they each shared with her a sense of duty and courage.

We must not forget Brynmenyn's former Reverend Henry Eynon Lewis, who befriended the Howell family and whose good deeds in the community of Brynmenyn were many. This gentleman's later life is described in an obituary entitled 'Well Known Welsh Figure' in which it is stated that he became '[Chief] Clerk to the Glamorgan Insurance Committee' in 1912 and continued in this post for thirty-three years. Referring to his earlier ministerial work, the article that appeared in the *South Wales Echo* of August 29th 1946[68] also states that 'he was ordained as a minister and served three churches in the Bridgend area.' In later life, he became 'treasurer of the Welsh Congregational Union and was a Deacon at the Ebenezer Welsh Congregational Church in Cardiff.' Then, in 1946 after a period of sickness,

---

66   Local Studies Librarian: Bath Central Library.
67   *The Times* Deaths of October 9th 1937:
      courtesy of the National Library of Wales.
68   Local Studies Librarian: Cardiff Central Library.

Reverend Eynon Lewis was laid to rest, aged eighty-one, and his burial was private.

It remains to say a few words about the schools where Sarah Jane served as a junior teacher, beginning in Bryncethin, where new premises were built in 1924 and where children today respond to the ambitious motto, *We have Great Expectations*. As regards Tynyrheol, the external appearance of this school has not, seemingly, altered with the passing years. Known as Ysgol Gynradd Tynyrheol, its message is equally encouraging, *Mae Ysgol Hapus yn Gweithio'n Galed*, meaning *A Happy School Works Hard*. A few miles away in Gilfach Goch, Abercerdin has also stood the test of time. It is there that teachers and pupils enjoy a tree-top location; and their motto, *Together We Can Do It,* still unites the close-knit community.

Meanwhile, Ynysawdre Parish Hall remains as Sarah Jane once remembered it: an asset to the modern community, hosting a variety of meetings and functions. However, nothing can bring back the cosiness of its former school days when everyone huddled around the little stove to keep warm – before a giant forward march led to the brand-new premises of today's Brynmenyn Primary School. How Sarah Jane must have looked forward to teaching there, just down the road from Abergarw. She would have given her heart and soul to the little school, just as it has given its heart and soul to her.

Brynmenyn Primary
– the Little School with a Big Heart

EVER SINCE Councillor David Thomas turned the key of the door officially to open Brynmenyn School in 1913, so many old values in education and in life have given way to modern tendencies. Nevertheless, throughout these years the little school has continued to occupy the same buildings and playground to the south of the village common. From Log Book entries[69] we learn that in early days the authorities stipulated that pupils had to have lessons within the area where they lived. Brynmenyn's patch was bordered by the river Ogmore on one side and the Pwllandras railway-bridge on the other, and this meant that pupils beyond these boundaries were schooled elsewhere.

During the Great War, widespread diseases such as diphtheria and tuberculosis were causing problems on the home front. With precious little good news to share, everyone's heart sunk further when Lusitania was torpedoed not many miles from the Irish coast. This beautiful sea liner became the victim of a German attack when providing a passenger service, just as it did when returning to Fishguard harbour during those last few days of

---

[69]   Extracts of the Log Book of Brynmenyn Council School Mixed and Infants (1910 – 1973), held at Brynmenyn Primary School.

Sarah Jane's life. How times had changed in a matter of years and this is highlighted now with war-related Log Book entries, alongside mention of a special tea for the school children and teachers arranged by George and Jennet:

> *July 21st 1915*
> [There was a] half-[day] holiday in the afternoon of this day – a treat given to the school children by Mr and Mrs Howell, Abergarw, which was very much appreciated.
>
> *December 10th 1915*
> [The] Head Teacher enlisted under Lord Derby's scheme in His Majesty's Forces.
>
> *June 29th 1917*
> [The] Head Teacher [is] absent this day attending a conference on War Savings at Cardiff ...
>
> *June 18th 1918*
> Half day holiday granted: visit of a tank to Bridgend.

The ending of war and Armistice Day came with a school holiday heralding a time of togetherness that bonded the people of a relieved nation. Not long afterwards, good news arrived for the suffragettes with the granting of women's voting rights – many believing that the contributions of women during the war served to tip the scales. During these times, Thomas David Johns remained the school headmaster, just as he had been years earlier when Sarah Jane was one of his ambitious young assistants.

Mr Johns experienced the momentous occasion in the early 1920s when a motor bus carrying the important officers of Ogmore and Garw Council became the first vehicle to proceed along the new Pandy Road.[70] That was some event: crowds spilling in from all directions, witnessing the beginning of a new chapter in village life. No doubt, Mr Johns appreciated this progress, and the beginning of the *Brynmenyn Star's* regular bus shuttles back and forth to Bridgend, which led to regular Sunday excursions running to Ogmore by Sea, Southerndown and Porthcawl.[71] Of course, Sarah Jane's drowning caused Mr Johns personal shock and sadness, but his words at the time were gracious, once saying of his former assistant that she 'was very much liked and quite a favourite amongst the scholars.' On June 10th 1927, when still in office, Mr Johns' days came to an end, as the copy Log Book entry held at Brynmenyn Primary School confirms:

> It is with grief that I write the report of the death of Head Teacher, Mr T.D. Johns, who passed away at 11p.m. this day.

Mr Isaac Williams was next in charge, steering the school through many interesting years leading up to and beyond World War II. As ever, the well-being of the children came first: the local Medical Officer conducting regular malnutrition surveys, whilst health talks were provided by other visitors to the school. There were some exciting school trips taking place at the time: to the Zoological Gardens in London; Windsor Castle, and the River Thames, whilst some

---

[70]   *South Wales News* of May 1st 1923 – held at Brynmenyn Primary School.
[71]   *A Short History of Brynmenyn 1820 – 1900* by Bill Lavis:
       Brynmenyn Primary School Records.

of the boys were attending summer camps in Pendine. With
the use of motor cars becoming more widespread, parents
were attending school 'road-safety' seminars – whilst, into
the late 1930s, Sarah Jane's sister, Margot, was visiting
America during school holidays to see her Uncle Thomas
who had emigrated overseas years earlier.

During World War II, nearby Bridgend was heavily
involved, providing vital munitions work and underground
storage facilities which attracted tens-of-thousands of
workers to the area, many being women. All of this took
place a mile up the road from the town's Island Farm,
where prisoners of war were billeted in long huts, and
where General Dwight D. Eisenhower, Supreme
Commander of the Allied Expeditionary Force, welcomed
American troops in 1944.[72]

In supporting the soldiers, regular 'Savings Weeks'
raised vast sums of money for Spitfires, tanks, and other war
essentials, thanks to public generosity that knew no bounds.
At this time Local Defence Volunteers guarded the
homeland, as Army Cadets and Air Training Corps
Squadrons emerged from the needs of the day. During these
painful years of heavy loss, of lives and dignity and so much
more, Brynmenyn School pupils and teachers experienced
gas masks and blackout-rule, as well as the distant drone of
enemy planes. But it survived with the help of military
personnel stationed in the village and a search light unit
positioned on the nearby Common. And, during the dreaded

---

[72]   *Bridgend 900* (D. Brown and Sons, Bridgend & Cowbridge 1993):
        Bridgend Library Services.

Blitz, Brynmenyn welcomed the company of visiting children from the cities, who enriched life and schooling in the village. Here are a few more Log Book entries[73]:

> *June 4th 1940*
> Sixty evacuees from South Deal Junior Mixed and Infants School were admitted to this school at 9 a.m. this morning. They were being taught by their own teachers.

> *June 17th 1940*
> School closed in the afternoon of this day. All the staff members were engaged in completing forms relating to over 300 evacuees who had assembled at Tondu Council School.

> *July 15th 1940*
> An Air Raid warning was given at about 10.20 a.m. this morning. The children who can reach a reasonably good shelter – for example, in their homes within a period of five minutes – were dispersed immediately. The rest were directed to take up the safest position available in the school building.

The next year in December 1941, His Royal Highness King George VI visited the Ogmore Valley. This memorable day saw Brynmenyn scholars joining children from neighbouring schools in giving a rousing welcome when lining the streets in Bryncethin. Amongst the crowds was David Edwards, the husband of Sarah Jane's sister, Katie, who, whilst being on duty as a war time volunteer within the community

---

[73] Brynmenyn Council School Mixed and Infants (1910 – 1973): Glamorgan Archive Services.

police constabulary and regaled in smart uniform, had the fond memory of the King saluting him as he and the Queen passed by. Here are further wartime entries:

> *July 30th 1943*
> Mr Morgan, a local police officer called at the school and showed incendiary bombs to all the children. He told them what to do if they found any.

> *July 10th 1944*
> Mr R.T. Winn is this week attending a Revision Course for Bomb Reconnaissance officers at Cardiff.

Then, the day arrived that everybody had prayed for in May 1945: Victory in Europe. During the morning, staff and pupils participated in a 'service of thanksgiving' before everyone went home for an extended break amounting to a day-and-a-half.

Not many years afterwards, Brynmenyn School, now under the headship of Cadifor Davies, held a celebration tea on June 3rd 1953 to mark the Coronation of Queen Elizabeth II. Then, a month later, a day's holiday was declared because Her Majesty Queen Elizabeth II was passing through South Wales. Of course, Brynmenyn was now used to street parties – just as Bridgend was used to dancing in the streets – with another occasion to trigger the flag-flying and roadside festivities being the Investiture of Charles as Prince of Wales in 1969.

In the following summer of 1970, as teachers and scholars prepared for decimalisation – the unthinkable happened. The beautiful bronze sculpture, the pride and

glory of the *Sarah Jane Howell Memorial* that sat so
magnificently upon its pedestal, was wrenched away by
wrongdoers. This left just the plaque of Sarah Jane and the
inscribed wording, which were both moved inside the
school premises. Time had certainly redefined the meaning
of respect and sincerity, at least in the way that it once
symbolised the simpler ways of earlier life. But, all was not
lost, and this behaviour changed little. Sarah Jane's great
deed was well known by now; indeed, she had already
become a legend in her own right.

It is with thanks to Brynmenyn Primary School that
memories of Sarah Jane have, remarkably, lived on for a full
century. And whilst the introduction of the Eleven Plus and
other changes brought to an end the district scholarship as
once fully enjoyed by neighbouring schools, the *Sarah Jane
Howell Award* has been anticipated with great interest at
Brynmenyn School every July, since 1949. It is equally
pleasing that the award is still valued highly today, when the
best all-round pupil in the senior year is recognised. And
amongst meritorious winners from the past, are former
pupils who may have shared a favourite tale *or confession*
about their former schooldays. Here is a small collection
from the school archives, a mixture of treasured memories,
starting with something out of the ordinary describing 'An
Eclipse *Eclipsed*:'

> A 'once in a lifetime' event which occurred, was an
> eclipse of the sun. Armed with pieces of smoked glass,
> so that we wouldn't harm our eyes, the whole school
> trooped out into the playground at the appointed hour.

Gradually it became darker and we all squinted upwards as the sun became completely obscured. It was an eerie moment. For once we all stopped talking, as it seemed to me that even the birds stopped singing as the sky went dark.

Suddenly, the deathly hush was pierced by a blood-curdling yell.

'Sir, sir, help, sir. I've cut my finger on my piece of glass!

We gathered round, shark-like, to catch a glimpse of the poor boy's blood. Daylight flooded back and we all returned to our classrooms.

Here is a story from a pupil who once misused the inkwells:

I was stood behind the blackboard for a whole afternoon because I dipped the wrong end of a boy's pen in the inkwell! Yes, we had inkwells in those days, and wooden pens with detachable nibs, which had to be dipped every few words, [whilst] ink monitors [would] clean and fill the ink wells regularly.

This tale describes an unexpected dinner-time incident:

The canteen was where we learned our first law of physics – that every action has an equal and opposite reaction. This we demonstrated when eight children sitting on a bench lean back at the same time; the bench will topple over with disastrous results!

These words explain the scene during downpours of rain ...

[There was] the smell of wet wool as we sat on the hot pipes in the corridors on rainy days. And there was the joy of finding real ice on our little bottles of milk in the winter, because a fridge was almost unheard of in those days.

Meanwhile, here we have a mention of Sarah Jane:

> My first teacher [Miss Margot Howell] was a sweet, kind, efficient spinster with whom I stayed for two or three years, the sister of Sarah Jane Howell. A stove with a real fire and a guard around it took place of honour in the corner of the classroom, where writing was produced on slate pieces with white chalk.

Finally, bringing this chapter to a close is a letter from Thomas Rees Williams that appeared in a newspaper cutting belonging to Sarah Jane's family. Mr Williams, from Llangeinor, remembers the importance of punctuality in a strict environment, whilst the headmaster tried his hardest to help each child pass the *Eleven-Plus*. Classes were made up of a mixture of around forty boys and girls, and, besides the *Three R's*, multiplication tables had their time and place. As regards woodwork lessons, these were held in the nearby village, and there were also regular excursions into the countryside to do drawing work. All the while, football, rugby and running were regular sporting activities.

Mr Williams went on to mention the daily break-time drink of milk which cost a halfpenny. At lunch time the scholars went home for a meal because there were no school dinners then and, during the Christmas period, the teachers brought gifts for the children to take home. This gentleman also remembers children waiting to meet Sarah Jane's sister, Margot, so that they could hold her hand while strolling to school each morning. And, as regards the story's heroine, Mr Williams knew about Sarah Jane's great deed, and what she will always mean to *Brynmenyn Primary — the Little School with a Big Heart.*

Tears in Heaven and a Final Tribute

CHRISTMAS WAS DRAWING NEARER when teachers, pupils, governors and guests walked towards Brynmenyn Primary School on the morning of Thursday December 15th 2011. The next day spelt the end of term: a time to enjoy the festivities of another mid winter's break with school activities sent fast-forward into the New Year. But, with business continuing as usual this day, a special Memorial Assembly was uppermost in everyone's mind as footsteps neared the entrance. The morning service marked the 100th anniversary of Sarah Jane's brave sacrifice, the day when Brynmenyn's world was turned upside-down, dating back to the torrential downpours of early December 1911. Now, on a dark morning brightened by bouts of intermittent sunshine, just as it had apparently been on that fateful day, everyone guessed that something special lay in store; and they were not disappointed. Brynmenyn School had prepared well and just as every young scholar knew about his or her former teacher, soon they were singing her praises, too.

For Sarah Jane's niece, Janet Moody, her daughter, Kathryn, and the author, Sarah Jane's great-nephew, it was a memorable moment as they ventured up the steep walkway leading to the school. To the right, the neat evergreen laurels blend with tall pine trees straight ahead,

offering the feel of a country lane leading up a steep track –
not in the least dissimilar to the old road to Llangeinor, and
not a mile from it either. On the left stands a short stone
wall, as if holding the bank in place where, interestingly, all
those years ago when the school began, the dangerous
condition of this slope worried the headmaster. He voiced
his concerns to Messrs John and David Thomas, the
Alderman and Councillor respectively, when they, too,
ascended the well-walked incline on a school visit in 1913.[74]
Is it possible, one might wonder, that the boys used this
bank as a slide, before the perimeter fence at the top and
the wall at the bottom ruled this dangerous activity out of
bounds?

About half way up the slope, the red brick pillars of the
local works lead to a flight of steps reaching to the higher
level of the school building. It is there in a prominent
pulpit-position that the Sarah Jane Memorial used to look
onto the open hills and dales. What a sight it must have
been from the road, shining in the midday sun, and what an
inspiration to a school so perennial and permanent, yet
focussed and forward-planning, too. Brynmenyn Primary is
as down-to-earth as the grass is green, rooted to an expanse
of common land where quarries and a nearby mine once
prospered and whose matted ferns today peep over the rear
wall as if watching that feet are kept firmly on the ground.

Inside the Central Hall – where two of the local school
managers engaged in friendly banter, if not disagreement,

---

[74]   Log Book extracts of Brynmenyn Mixed and Infants School
        (1910 – 1973) held at Brynmenyn School.

about children's attitudes way back in 1913 – there was a feeling of peace and harmony. Amongst a sea of intelligent, smiling, young faces, naturally endorsing today's school motto *The Best Wealth is Knowledge (Goreu Cyfoeth Gwybodaeth)*, the senior scholars assembled on the stage, whilst the younger children sat shoulder-to-shoulder covering the wooden block floor. It was a delightful scene of colour and of life, set against the shapes and patterns that adorned the solid walls that shut-out the worries and concerns of the outside world. At the loftier levels near the ceiling, generous windows still offer a prism of light through which all the colours of the rainbow have been cascaded down through the years – onto a scene where the Reverend Eynon Lewis once commanded centre stage, and where Sarah Jane was meant to teach. How sad this never happened, but equally how comforting to see her photographs on the wall, telling the story of a beautiful, brave and forever-young heroine who still flies the flag for this little school.

It must have been a proud moment for Mrs Clare Dale to conduct this service as the ninth Head Teacher to have carried the school baton into the future. When paying her personal respect to Sarah Jane, she no doubt echoed the sentiments of her predecessors, who had not only preserved their former colleague's memory, but had probably laid flowers on her grave, just as the current teachers and pupils had done days earlier. It is this commitment and respect that still fuels the school's warm hearth, where coal from the local seams once burnt to a red-hot glow as bracken from the Common glistened in the frost capped snow. Over the years, many teachers played their part just as their senior 'Heads' led the way.

As for the highlight of the service, this was when young Nico Fitzgibbon was invited onto the stage. Nico, a former pupil and singer, stepped forward to enthral his audience this day. *Tears in Heaven* is a well-loved ballad written by Eric Clapton and Will Jennings. It is set to the steady beat and pace that is befitting of Brynmenyn around the time when Jenkin Morgan and his father, Evan, cut the corn with a scythe, or even later when boys whiled away hot summer afternoons watching village batsmen facing the wayward bowls of a bumpy wicket. But its melody, words and gentle rhythm are enough to pull heart strings across the widest oceans and throughout the ageless years. As Nico's rendition filled the room with a peaceful sadness, he took us back in time, with a performance that everyone enjoyed and no one will forget:

> Would you know my name
> If I saw you in Heaven?
> Would it be the same
> If I saw you in...[75]

In such an atmosphere as this, we can be forgiven for putting our own lives under the scrutiny and examination of our personal thoughts, concerns and perplexities, as our existences flash by in front of our eyes. We are all the same, possessed of these incredible built-in mechanisms that work

---

[75]   Web site: www. Eric Clapton *Tears in Heaven* Lyrics, as at June 30th 2014.

for each of us in differing degrees. Life can be a complicated mix, too, full of challenges to surmount and not always easy ones. No doubt, Sarah Jane found her world to be much the same, as did the song's musical directors who composed these beautiful, but sad, words at a time when Mr Clapton was coming to terms with the tragic passing of his young son. [76]

Down through the years, music has enriched the spirit of us all, penetrating deeply into the inner sanctums of our being, where we hope for peace. This is our treasure, to protect at all times, mindful of our changing place in this wonderful but challenging world. Here are more words from Nico as he brought to an end this touching ballad:

> Beyond the door there's peace I'm sure.
> And I know there'll be no more tears in Heaven.

And so the final words about our young heroine, who died aged twenty-one, describe the centenary celebrations of her most noble act. So many compliments have been paid throughout the years that Sarah Jane's popularity will live on. Indeed, this was the exact message from the late minister and poet, William Evans (1883 – 1968), but better known as bard Wil Ifan – when he presented a BBC radio programme many years ago, entitled 'Pum Munud Y Plant' ('Five Minutes for the Children'). Introducing the village of Brynmenyn, he explained the part Sarah Jane played in its history, mentioning that each time he passed through the village, he looked-up at the school where the bronze sculpture in her honour caught his eye.

---

[76]   Web site: www. Eric Clapton Wikipedia, as at June 30th 2014.

This gentleman explained that Sarah Jane was not born into high society or even overt privilege, but was merely an ordinary young school teacher. Yet memories of her drowning whilst trying to help a pupil to safety continue to teach everyone an unforgettable lesson. Here are some of his words, the final tribute to Sarah Jane... 'The Welsh Heroine'... 'Yr Arwres Cymraes'... wrapped-up in a humbling message to us all:

> You and I would say she finished her career as a teacher almost before it had started. But I am not so sure, for as long as the memorial exists, and indeed years after it will have disappeared, the little heroine will continue to teach us how endearing bravery can be so true ...
>
> What a large class! And every one of us needs to learn the lesson that comes from her quiet lips.

~ Finis ~

ABOUT THE AUTHOR

ROGER PENN is a native of Whitland, Carmarthenshire, where he attended the local primary and grammar schools before joining Lloyds Bank Limited in 1976. After a 34 year career serving in many branches across South Wales, Roger retired in January 2010 still a believer in the traditional bank values of old.

As a student of the written word, Roger now dedicates more time to writing having gained great satisfaction from his first two titles, *Dolycwrt – the Days of a Country Doctor's Surgery* – which describes a century of life, traditional medicine and community events as seen by Dolycwrt Surgery in Whitland – and *Beyond the Call of Duty*, a biography of his father, 'Whitland's Dr Penn.'

Roger, a former Welsh Rugby Union referee, has also completed a sporting history and this follows a research tour he made to New Zealand in 2012. *Three Feathers and a Silver Fern* describes the off-field events of 'Wales and the All Blacks' from the first meeting of the two rugby nations in 1905 to date, and it is proving to be another popular read.